Global Population Issues, Grade 7

T0316379

What if you could challenge your seventh-grade students to explore mathematical principles as well as global population issues as they consider population density? With this volume in the *STEM Road Map Curriculum Series*, you can!

Global Population Issues outlines a journey that will steer your students toward authentic problem solving while grounding them in integrated STEM disciplines. Like the other volumes in the series, this book is designed to meet the growing need to infuse real-world learning into K–12 classrooms.

This interdisciplinary, four-lesson module uses project- and problem-based learning to help students to devise a model for counting populations of a given species on Earth and develop a formal presentation of their models for consideration by a panel of experts. Students will examine species' ecosystems, explore global populations with an economic and geographical lens, take on the role of an urban planner to develop a megacity that incorporates what they have researched and learned about the consequences of population density and overpopulation, and share literature relevant to their applied species model.

To support this goal, students will do the following:

- Explore how to gather information about a population and make valid generalizations and inferences from this information

- Utilize mathematical practices to complete mathematical explorations

- Explore the impact of population density on humans and the environment

- Communicate learning and experiences about population density and its influence on humans and the environment through various forms of writing, speaking, and analyzing non-fiction text

- Explore the historical, social, geographical, and economic factors related to population density

The *STEM Road Map Curriculum Series* is anchored in the Next Generation Science Standards, the Common Core State Standards, and the Framework for 21st Century Learning. In-depth and flexible, *Global Population Issues* can be used as a whole unit or in part to meet the needs of districts, schools, and teachers who are charting a course toward an integrated STEM approach.

Carla C. Johnson is a Professor of Science Education and Office of Research and Innovation Faculty Research Fellow at North Carolina State University, North Carolina, USA.

Janet B. Walton is a Senior Research Scholar at North Carolina State's College of Education in Raleigh, North Carolina, USA.

Erin E. Peters-Burton is the Donna R. and David E. Sterling Endowed Professor in Science Education at George Mason University in Fairfax, Virginia, USA.

THE STEM ROAD MAP CURRICULUM SERIES

Series editors: Carla C. Johnson, Janet B. Walton, and Erin E. Peters-Burton

Map out a journey that will steer your students toward authentic problem solving as you ground them in integrated STEM disciplines.

Co-published by Routledge and NSTA Press, in partnership with the National Science Teaching Association, this K–12 curriculum series is anchored in the Next Generation Science Standards, the Common Core State Standards, and the Framework for 21st Century Learning. It was developed to meet the growing need to infuse real-world STEM learning into classrooms.

Each book is an in-depth module that uses project- and problem-based learning. First, your students are presented with a challenge. Then, they apply what they learn using science, social studies, English language arts, and mathematics. Engaging and flexible, each volume can be used as a whole unit or in part to meet the needs of districts, schools, and teachers who are charting a course toward an integrated STEM approach.

Modules are available from NSTA Press and Routledge, and organized under the following themes. For an update listing of the volumes in the series, please visit *www.routledge.com/STEM-Road-Map-Curriculum-Series/book-series/SRM* (for titles co-published by Routledge and NSTA Press), or *www.nsta.org/book-series/stem-road-map-curriculum* (for titles published by NSTA Press).

Co-published by Routledge and NSTA Press:
Optimizing the Human Experience:

- *Our Changing Environment, Grade K: STEM Road Map for Elementary School*
- *Genetically Modified Organisms, Grade 7: STEM Road Map for Middle School*
- *Rebuilding the Natural Environment, Grade 10: STEM Road Map for High School*
- *Mineral Resources, Grade 11: STEM Road Map for High School*

Cause and Effect:

- *Formation of the Earth, Grade 9: STEM Road Map for High School*

Sustainable Systems:

- *Composting, Grade 5: STEM Road Map for Elementary School*
- *Global Population Issues, Grade 7: STEM Road Map for Middle School*
- *The Speed of Green, Grade 8: STEM Road Map for Middle School*
- *Creating Global Bonds, Grade 12: STEM Road Map for High School*

Published by NSTA Press:
Innovation and Progress:

- *Amusement Park of the Future, Grade 6: STEM Road Map for Elementary School*
- *Transportation in the Future, Grade 3: STEM Road Map for Elementary School*
- *Harnessing Solar Energy, Grade 4: STEM Road Map for Elementary School*
- *Wind Energy, Grade 5: STEM Road Map for Elementary School*

- *Construction Materials, Grade 11: STEM Road Map for High School*

The Represented World:

- *Patterns and the Plant World, Grade 1: STEM Road Map for Elementary School*
- *Investigating Environmental Changes, Grade 2: STEM Road Map for Elementary School*
- *Swing Set Makeover, Grade 3: STEM Road Map for Elementary School*
- *Rainwater Analysis, Grade 5: STEM Road Map for Elementary School*
- *Packaging Design, Grade 6: STEM Road Map for Middle School*
- *Improving Bridge Design, Grade 8: STEM Road Map for Middle School*
- *Radioactivity, Grade 11: STEM Road Map for High School*
- *Car Crashes, Grade 12: STEM Road Map for High School*

Cause and Effect:

- *Physics in Motion, Grade K: STEM Road Map for Elementary School*
- *Influence of Waves, Grade 1: STEM Road Map for Elementary School*
- *Natural Hazards, Grade 2: STEM Road Map for Elementary School*
- *Human Impacts on Our Climate, Grade 6: STEM Road Map for Middle School*
- *The Changing Earth, Grade 8: STEM Road Map for Middle School*
- *Healthy Living, Grade 10: STEM Road Map for High School*

Global Population Issues

Grade
7

STEM Road Map
for Middle School

Edited by Carla C. Johnson, Janet B. Walton, and
Erin E. Peters-Burton

Routledge
Taylor & Francis Group

NEW YORK AND LONDON

nsta Press
National Science Teaching Association

Designed cover image: © Getty Images and © Shutterstock

First published 2024
by Routledge
605 Third Avenue, New York, NY 10158

and by Routledge
4 Park Square, Milton Park, Abingdon, Oxon, OX14 4RN

Routledge is an imprint of the Taylor & Francis Group, an informa business

A co-publication with NSTA Press

Routledge is committed to publishing material that promotes the best in inquiry-based science education. However, conditions of actual use may vary, and the safety procedures and practices described in this book are intended to serve only as a guide. Additional precautionary measures may be required. Routledge and the authors do not warrant or represent that the procedures and practices in this book meet any safety code or standard of federal, state, or local regulations. Routledge and the authors disclaim any liability for personal injury or damage to property arising out of or relating to the use of this book, including any of the recommendations, instructions, or materials contained therein.

Trademark notice: Product or corporate names may be trademarks or registered trademarks, and are used only for identification and explanation without intent to infringe.

Library of Congress Cataloging-in-Publication Data
Names: Johnson, Carla C., 1969- editor. | Walton, Janet B., 1968–, editor. | Peters-Burton, Erin E., editor.
Title: Global population issues, grade 7 : STEM road map for middle school / edited by Carla C. Johnson, Janet B. Walton, and Erin E. Peters-Burton.
Description: First edition. | New York : Routledge, 2024. |
Series: STEM road map curriculum series | Includes bibliographical references and index.
Identifiers: LCCN 2023006399 (print) | LCCN 2023006400 (ebook) | ISBN 9781032441641 (hbk) |
ISBN 9781032431208 (pbk) | ISBN 9781003370789 (ebk)
Subjects: LCSH: Population density—Study and teaching (Middle school) | Project method in teaching. |
Problem-based learning.
Classification: LCC HB1953 .G563 2024 (print) | LCC HB1953 (ebook) | DDC 304.6/1—dc23/eng/20230531
LC record available at https://lccn.loc.gov/2023006399
LC ebook record available at https://lccn.loc.gov/2023006400

ISBN: 978-1-032-44164-1 (hbk)
ISBN: 978-1-032-43120-8 (pbk)
ISBN: 978-1-003-37078-9 (ebk)

DOI: 10.4324/9781003370789

Typeset in Palatino
by codeMantra

CONTENTS

Part 1: The STEM Road Map: Background, Theory, and Practice

Part 2: Global Population Issues: STEM Road Map Module

CONTENTS

④ **Global Population Issues Lesson Plans**

*Adrienne Redmond-Sanogo, Juliana Utley, Toni Ivey,
Sue Christian Parsons, Janet B. Walton, Carla C. Johnson,
and Erin E. Peters-Burton*

CONTENTS

ABOUT THE EDITORS AND AUTHORS

Dr. Carla C. Johnson is a Professor of Science Education and Office of Research and Innovation Faculty Research Fellow at NC State University. Dr. Johnson has served (2015–2021) as the director of research and evaluation for the Department of Defense–funded Army Educational Outreach Program (AEOP), a global portfolio of STEM education programs, competitions, and apprenticeships. She has been a leader in STEM education for the past decade, serving as the director of STEM Centers, editor of the *School Science and Mathematics* journal, and lead researcher for the evaluation of Tennessee's Race to the Top–funded STEM portfolio. Dr. Johnson has published over 200 articles, books, book chapters, and curriculum books focused on STEM education. She is a former science and social studies teacher and was the recipient of the 2013 Outstanding Science Teacher Educator of the Year award from the Association for Science Teacher Education (ASTE), the 2012 Award for Excellence in Integrating Science and Mathematics from the School Science and Mathematics Association (SSMA), the 2014 award for best paper on Implications of Research for Educational Practice from ASTE, and the 2006 Outstanding Early Career Scholar Award from SSMA. Her research focuses on STEM education policy implementation, effective science teaching, and integrated STEM approaches.

Dr. Janet B. Walton is a senior research scholar at NC State's College of Education in Raleigh, North Carolina. Her research focus includes collaboration between schools and community stakeholders for STEM education, problem- and project- based learning pedagogies, online learning, and mixed methods research methodologies. She leverages her workforce development and leadership background to bring contextual STEM experiences into the classroom and provide students and educators with innovative resources and curricular materials. She is the former assistant director of evaluation of research and evaluation for the Department of Defense–funded Army Educational Outreach Program (AEOP), a global portfolio of STEM education programs, competitions, and apprenticeships, and specializes in evaluation of STEM programs.

Dr. Erin E. Peters-Burton is the Donna R. and David E. Sterling endowed professor in science education at George Mason University in Fairfax, Virginia. She uses her experiences from 15 years as an engineer and secondary science, engineering, and mathematics teacher to develop research projects that directly inform classroom practice in science and engineering. Her research agenda is based on the idea that all students should build self-awareness of how they learn science and engineering. She works to help students see themselves as "science-minded" and help teachers create classrooms that support student skills to develop scientific knowledge. To accomplish this, she pursues research projects that investigate ways that students and teachers can use self-regulated learning theory in science and engineering, as well as how inclusive STEM schools can help students succeed. She received the Outstanding Science Teacher Educator of the Year award from ASTE in 2016 and a Teacher of Distinction Award and a Scholarly Achievement Award from George Mason University in 2012, and in 2010 she was named University Science Educator of the Year by the Virginia Association of Science Teachers.

Dr. Toni A. Ivey is an associate professor of science education in the College of Education at Oklahoma State University. A former science teacher, Dr. Ivey's research is focused on science and STEM education for students and teachers across K-20.

Dr. Toni A. May is an associate professor of assessment, research, and statistics in the School of Education at Drexel University in Philadelphia. Dr. May's research concentrates on assessment and evaluation in education, with a focus on K–12 STEM.

Dr. Tamara J. Moore is an associate professor of engineering education in the College of Engineering at Purdue University. Dr. Moore's research focuses on defining STEM integration through the use of engineering as the connection and investigating its power for student learning.

Dr. Sue Christian Parsons is an associate professor and the Jacques Munroe Professor in Reading and Literacy Education at Oklahoma State University. A former English/language arts teacher, her research focuses on teacher development and teaching and advocating for diverse learners through literature for children and young adults.

Dr. Adrienne A. Redmond-Sanogo is an assistant professor of mathematics education in the College of Education at Oklahoma State University. Dr. Redmond-Sanogo's research is focused on mathematics and STEM education across K–12 and preservice teacher education.

Dr. Juliana Utley is an associate professor and Morsani Chair in Mathematics Education in the College of Education at Oklahoma State University. A former mathematics teacher, Dr. Utley's research is focused on mathematics and STEM education across K–12.

John Weaver is a clinical instructor in the College of Education at Oklahoma State University. A former mathematics teacher, Weaver teaches elementary and secondary mathematics methods courses and is a Master Teacher for the OSUTeach program.

ACKNOWLEDGMENTS

This module was developed as part of the STEM Road Map Project (Carla C. Johnson, principal investigator). The Purdue University College of Education, General Motors, and other sources provided funding for this project.

See *www.routledge.com/9781138804234* for more information about *STEM Road Map: A Framework for Integrated STEM Education.*

PART 1

THE STEM ROAD MAP

BACKGROUND, THEORY, AND PRACTICE

OVERVIEW OF THE *STEM ROAD MAP* CURRICULUM SERIES

Carla C. Johnson, Erin Peters-Burton, and Tamara J. Moore

The *STEM Road Map Curriculum Series* was conceptualized and developed by a team of STEM educators from across the United States in response to a growing need to infuse real-world learning contexts, delivered through authentic problem-solving pedagogy, into K–12 classrooms. The curriculum series is grounded in integrated STEM, which focuses on the integration of the STEM disciplines – science, technology, engineering, and mathematics – delivered across content areas, incorporating the Framework for 21st Century Learning along with grade-level-appropriate academic standards. The curriculum series begins in kindergarten, with a five-week instructional sequence that introduces students to the STEM themes and gives them grade-level-appropriate topics and real-world challenges or problems to solve. The series uses project-based and problem-based learning, presenting students with the problem or challenge during the first lesson, and then teaching them science, social studies, English language arts, mathematics, and other content, as they apply what they learn to the challenge or problem at hand.

Authentic assessment and differentiation are embedded throughout the modules. Each *STEM Road Map Curriculum Series* module has a lead discipline, which may be science, social studies, English language arts, or mathematics. All disciplines are integrated into each module, along with ties to engineering. Another key component is the use of STEM Research Notebooks to allow students to track their own learning progress. The modules are designed with a scaffolded approach, with increasingly complex concepts and skills introduced as students progress through grade levels.

The developers of this work view the curriculum as a resource that is intended to be used either as a whole or in part to meet the needs of districts, schools, and teachers who are implementing an integrated STEM approach. A variety of implementation formats are possible, from using one stand-alone module at a given grade level to using all five modules to provide 25 weeks of instruction. Also, within each grade band (K–2, 3–5, 6–8, 9–12), the modules can be sequenced in various ways to suit specific needs.

Carla C. Johnson et al.

STANDARDS-BASED APPROACH

The *STEM Road Map Curriculum Series* is anchored in the *Next Generation Science Standards* (*NGSS*), the *Common Core State Standards for Mathematics* (*CCSS Mathematics*), the *Common Core State Standards for English Language Arts* (*CCSS ELA*), and the Framework for 21st Century Learning. Each module includes a detailed curriculum map that incorporates the associated standards from the particular area correlated to lesson plans. The STEM Road Map has very clear and strong connections to these academic standards, and each of the grade-level topics was derived from the mapping of the standards to ensure alignment among topics, challenges or problems, and the required academic standards for students. Therefore, the curriculum series takes a standards-based approach and is designed to provide authentic contexts for application of required knowledge and skills.

THEMES IN THE *STEM ROAD MAP CURRICULUM SERIES*

The K–12 STEM Road Map is organized around five real-world STEM themes that were generated through an examination of the big ideas and challenges for society included in STEM standards and those that are persistent dilemmas for current and future generations:

- Cause and Effect

- Innovation and Progress

- The Represented World

- Sustainable Systems

- Optimizing the Human Experience

These themes are designed as springboards for launching students into an exploration of real-world learning situated within big ideas. Most important, the five STEM Road Map themes serve as a framework for scaffolding STEM learning across the K–12 continuum.

The themes are distributed across the STEM disciplines so that they represent the big ideas in science (Cause and Effect; Sustainable Systems), technology (Innovation and Progress; Optimizing the Human Experience), engineering (Innovation and Progress; Sustainable Systems; Optimizing the Human Experience), and mathematics (The Rep- resented World), as well as concepts and challenges in social studies and 21st century skills that are also excellent contexts for learning in English language arts. The process of developing themes began with the clustering of the *NGSS* performance expectations and the National Academy of Engineering's grand challenges for engineering, which led to the development of the challenge in each module and connections of the module activities to the *CCSS Mathematics* and *CCSS ELA* standards.

We performed these mapping processes with large teams of experts and found that these five themes provided breadth, depth, and coherence to frame a high-quality STEM learning experience from kindergarten through 12th grade.

Cause and Effect

The concept of cause and effect is a powerful and pervasive notion in the STEM fields. It is the foundation of understanding how and why things happen as they do. Humans spend considerable effort and resources trying to understand the causes and effects of natural and designed phenomena to gain better control over events and the environment and to be prepared to react appropriately. Equipped with the knowledge of a specific cause-and-effect relationship, we can lead better lives or contribute to the community by altering the cause, leading to a different effect. For example, if a person recognizes that irresponsible energy consumption leads to global climate change, that person can act to remedy his or her contribution to the situation. Although cause and effect is a core idea in the STEM fields, it can actually be difficult to determine. Students should be capable of understanding not only when evidence points to cause and effect but also when evidence points to relationships but not direct causality. The major goal of education is to foster students to be empowered, analytic thinkers, capable of thinking through complex processes to make important decisions. Understanding causality, as well as when it cannot be determined, will help students become better consumers, global citizens, and community members.

Innovation and Progress

One of the most important factors in determining whether humans will have a positive future is innovation. Innovation is the driving force behind progress, which helps create possibilities that did not exist before. Innovation and progress are creative entities, but in the STEM fields, they are anchored by evidence and logic, and they use established concepts to move the STEM fields forward. In creating something new, students must consider what is already known in the STEM fields and apply this knowledge appropriately. When we innovate, we create value that was not there previously and create new conditions and possibilities for even more innovations. Students should consider how their innovations might affect progress and use their STEM thinking to change current human burdens to benefits. For example, if we develop more efficient cars that use by-products from another manufacturing industry, such as food processing, then we have used waste productively and reduced the need for the waste to be hauled away, an indirect benefit of the innovation.

The Represented World

When we communicate about the world we live in, how the world works, and how we can meet the needs of humans, sometimes we can use the actual phenomena to

Carla C. Johnson et al.

explain a concept. Sometimes, however, the concept is too big, too slow, too small, too fast, or too complex for us to explain using the actual phenomena, and we must use a representation or a model to help communicate the important features. We need representations and models such as graphs, tables, mathematical expressions, and diagrams because it makes our thinking visible. For example, when examining geologic time, we cannot actually observe the passage of such large chunks of time, so we create a timeline or a model that uses a proportional scale to visually illustrate how much time has passed for different eras. Another example may be something too complex for students at a particular grade level, such as explaining the *p* subshell orbitals of electrons to fifth graders. Instead, we use the Bohr model, which more closely represents the orbiting of planets and is accessible to fifth graders.

When we create models, they are helpful because they point out the most important features of a phenomenon. We also create representations of the world with mathematical functions, which help us change parameters to suit the situation. Creating representations of a phenomenon engages students because they are able to identify the important features of that phenomenon and communicate them directly. But because models are estimates of a phenomenon, they leave out some of the details, so it is important for students to evaluate their usefulness as well as their shortcomings.

Sustainable Systems

From an engineering perspective, the term *system* refers to the use of "concepts of component need, component interaction, systems interaction, and feedback. The interaction of subcomponents to produce a functional system is a common lens used by all engineering disciplines for understanding, analysis, and design" (Koehler et al., 2013, p. 8). Systems can be either open (e.g., an ecosystem) or closed (e.g., a car battery). Ideally, a system should be sustainable, able to maintain equilibrium without much energy from outside the structure. Looking at a garden, we see flowers blooming, weeds sprouting, insects buzzing, and various forms of life living within its boundaries. This is an example of an ecosystem, a collection of living organisms that survive together, functioning as a system. The interaction of the organisms within the system and the influences of the environment (e.g., water, sunlight) can maintain the system for a period of time, thus demonstrating its ability to endure. Sustainability is a desirable feature of a system because it allows for existence of the entity in the long term.

In the STEM Road Map project, we identified different standards that we consider to be oriented toward systems that students should know and understand in the K–12 setting. These include ecosystems, the rock cycle, Earth processes (such as erosion, tectonics, ocean currents, weather phenomena), Earth-Sun-Moon cycles, heat transfer, and the interaction among the geosphere, biosphere, hydrosphere, and atmosphere. Students and teachers should understand that we live in a world of systems that are not independent of each other, but rather are intrinsically linked such that a disruption in one part of a system will have reverberating effects on other parts of the system.

Optimizing the Human Experience

Science, technology, engineering, and mathematics as disciplines have the capacity to continuously improve the ways humans live, interact, and find meaning in the world, thus working to optimize the human experience. This idea has two components: being more suited to our environment and being more fully human. For example, the progression of STEM ideas can help humans create solutions to complex problems, such as improving ways to access water sources, designing energy sources with minimal impact on our environment, developing new ways of communication and expression, and building efficient shelters. STEM ideas can also provide access to the secrets and wonders of nature. Learning in STEM requires students to think logically and systematically, which is a way of knowing the world that is markedly different from knowing the world as an artist. When students can employ various ways of knowing and understand when it is appropriate to use a different way of knowing or integrate ways of knowing, they are fully experiencing the best of what it is to be human. The problem-based learning scenarios provided in the STEM Road Map help students develop ways of thinking like STEM professionals as they ask questions and design solutions. They learn to optimize the human experience by innovating improvements in the designed world in which they live.

THE NEED FOR AN INTEGRATED STEM APPROACH

At a basic level, STEM stands for science, technology, engineering, and mathematics. Over the past decade, however, STEM has evolved to have a much broader scope and implications. Now, educators and policy makers refer to STEM as not only a concentrated area for investing in the future of the United States and other nations but also as a domain and mechanism for educational reform.

The good intentions of the recent decade-plus of focus on accountability and increased testing has resulted in significant decreases not only in instructional time for teaching science and social studies but also in the flexibility of teachers to promote authentic, problem-solving–focused classroom environments. The shift has had a detrimental impact on student acquisition of vitally important skills, which many refer to as 21st century skills, and often the ability of students to "think." Further, schooling has become increasingly siloed into compartments of mathematics, science, English language arts, and social studies, lacking any of the connections that are overwhelmingly present in the real world around children. Students have experienced school as content provided in boxes that must be memorized, devoid of any real-world context, and often have little understanding of why they are learning these things.

STEM-focused projects, curriculum, activities, and schools have emerged as a means to address these challenges. However, most of these efforts have continued to focus on the individual STEM disciplines (predominantly science and engineering) through more STEM classes and after-school programs in a "STEM-enhanced" approach (Breiner et al., 2012). But in traditional and STEM-enhanced approaches, there is little to

no focus on other disciplines that are integral to the context of STEM in the real world. Integrated STEM education, on the other hand, infuses the learning of important STEM content and concepts with a much-needed emphasis on 21st century skills and a problem- and project-based pedagogy that more closely mirrors the real-world setting for society's challenges. It incorporates social studies, English language arts, and the arts as pivotal and necessary (Johnson, 2013; Rennie et al., 2012; Roehrig et al., 2012).

FRAMEWORK FOR STEM INTEGRATION IN THE CLASSROOM

The *STEM Road Map Curriculum Series* is grounded in the Framework for STEM Integration in the Classroom as conceptualized by Moore, Guzey, and Brown (2014) and Moore et al. (2014). The framework has six elements, described in the context of how they are used in the *STEM Road Map Curriculum Series* as follows:

1. The STEM Road Map contexts are meaningful to students and provide motivation to engage with the content. Together, these allow students to have different ways to enter into the challenge.

2. The STEM Road Map modules include engineering design that allows students to design technologies (i.e., products that are part of the designed world) for a compelling purpose.

3. The STEM Road Map modules provide students with the opportunities to learn from failure and redesign based on the lessons learned.

4. The STEM Road Map modules include standards-based disciplinary content as the learning objectives.

5. The STEM Road Map modules include student-centered pedagogies that allow students to grapple with the content, tie their ideas to the context, and learn to think for themselves as they deepen their conceptual knowledge.

6. The STEM Road Map modules emphasize 21st century skills and, in particular, highlight communication and teamwork.

All of the STEM Road Map modules incorporate these six elements; however, the level of emphasis on each of these elements varies based on the challenge or problem in each module.

THE NEED FOR THE *STEM ROAD MAP CURRICULUM SERIES*

As focus is increasing on integrated STEM, and additional schools and programs decide to move their curriculum and instruction in this direction, there is a need for

high-quality, research-based curriculum designed with integrated STEM at the core. Several good resources are available to help teachers infuse engineering or more STEM-enhanced approaches, but no curriculum exists that spans K–12 with an integrated STEM focus. The next chapter provides detailed information about the specific pedagogy, instructional strategies, and learning theory on which the *STEM Road Map Curriculum Series* is grounded.

REFERENCES

Breiner, J., Harkness, M., Johnson, C. C., & Koehler, C. (2012). What is STEM? A discussion about conceptions of STEM in education and partnerships. *School Science and Mathematics*, *112*(1), 3–11.

Johnson, C. C. (2013). Conceptualizing integrated STEM education: Editorial. *School Science and Mathematics*, *113*(8), 367–368.

Koehler, C. M., Bloom, M. A., & Binns, I. C. (2013). Lights, camera, action: Developing a methodology to document mainstream films' portrayal of nature of science and scientific inquiry. *Electronic Journal of Science Education*, *17*(2).

Moore, T. J., Guzey, S. S., & Brown, A. (2014). Greenhouse design to increase habitable land: An engineering unit. *Science Scope*, *37*(7), 51–57.

Moore, T. J., Stohlmann, M. S., Wang, H.-H., Tank, K. M., Glancy, A. W., & Roehrig, G. H. (2014). Implementation and integration of engineering in K–12 STEM education. In S. Purzer, J. Strobel, & M. Cardella (Eds.), *Engineering in pre-college settings: Synthesizing research, policy, and practices* (pp. 35–60). Purdue Press.

Rennie, L., Venville, G., & Wallace, J. (2012). *Integrating science, technology, engineering, and mathematics: Issues, reflections, and ways forward*. Routledge.

Roehrig, G. H., Moore, T. J., Wang, H. H., & Park, M. S. (2012). Is adding the E enough? Investigating the impact of K–12 engineering standards on the implementation of STEM integration. *School Science and Mathematics*, *112*(1), 31–44.

STRATEGIES USED IN THE *STEM ROAD MAP CURRICULUM SERIES*

Erin Peters-Burton, Carla C. Johnson, Toni A. May, and Tamara J. Moore

The *STEM Road Map Curriculum Series* uses what has been identified through research as best-practice pedagogy, including embedded formative assessment strategies throughout each module. This chapter briefly describes the key strategies that are employed in the series.

PROJECT- AND PROBLEM-BASED LEARNING

Each module in the *STEM Road Map Curriculum Series* uses either project-based learning or problem-based learning to drive the instruction. Project-based learning begins with a driving question to guide student teams in addressing a contextualized local or community problem or issue. The outcome of project-based instruction is a product that is conceptualized, designed, and tested through a series of scaffolded learning experiences (Blumenfeld et al., 1991; Krajcik & Blumenfeld, 2006). Problem-based learning is often grounded in a fictitious scenario, challenge, or problem (Barell, 2006; Lambros, 2004). On the first day of instruction within the unit, student teams are provided with the context of the problem. Teams work through a series of activities and use open-ended research to develop their potential solution to the problem or challenge, which need not be a tangible product (Johnson, 2003).

ENGINEERING DESIGN PROCESS

The *STEM Road Map Curriculum Series* uses engineering design as a way to facilitate integrated STEM within the modules. The engineering design process (EDP) is depicted in Figure 2.1 (p. 12). It highlights two major aspects of engineering design – problem scoping and solution generation – and six specific components of working toward a design: define the problem, learn about the problem, plan a solution, try the solution, test the solution, decide whether the solution is good enough. It also shows

Figure 2.1 Engineering Design Process

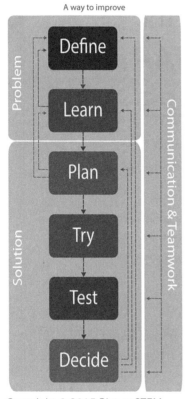

that communication and teamwork are involved throughout the entire process. As the arrows in the figure indicate, the order in which the components of engineering design are addressed depends on what becomes needed as designers progress through the EDP. Designers must communicate and work in teams throughout the process. The EDP is iterative, meaning that components of the process can be repeated as needed until the design is good enough to present to the client as a potential solution to the problem.

Problem scoping is the process of gathering and analyzing information to deeply understand the engineering design problem. It includes defining the problem and learning about the problem. Defining the problem includes identifying the problem, the client, and the end user of the design. The client is the person (or people) who hired the designers to do the work, and the end user is the person (or people) who will use the final design. The designers must also identify the criteria and the constraints of the problem. The criteria are the things the client wants from the solution, and the constraints are the things that limit the possible solutions. The designers must spend significant time learning about the problem, which can include activities such as the following:

- Reading informational texts and researching about relevant concepts or contexts

- Identifying and learning about needed mathematical and scientific skills, knowledge, and tools

- Learning about things done previously to solve similar problems

- Experimenting with possible materials that could be used in the design

Problem scoping also allows designers to consider how to measure the success of the design in addressing specific criteria and staying within the constraints over multiple iterations of solution generation.

Solution generation includes planning a solution, trying the solution, testing the solution, and deciding whether the solution is good enough. Planning the solution includes generating many design ideas that both address the criteria and meet the constraints. Here the designers must consider what was learned about the problem during problem scoping. Design plans include clear communication of design ideas through media such as notebooks, blueprints, schematics, or storyboards. They also include details about the design, such as measurements, materials, colors, costs of materials, instructions for how things fit together, and sets of directions. Making the decision about which design idea to move forward involves considering the trade-offs of each design idea.

Once a clear design plan is in place, the designers must try the solution. Trying the solution includes developing a prototype (a testable model) based on the plan generated. The prototype might be something physical or a process to accomplish a goal. This component of design requires that the designers consider the risk involved in implementing the design. The prototype developed must be tested. Testing the solution includes conducting fair tests that verify whether the plan is a solution that is good enough to meet the client and end user needs and wants. Data need to be collected about the results of the tests of the prototype, and these data should be used to make evidence-based decisions regarding the design choices made in the plan. Here, the designers must again consider the criteria and constraints for the problem.

Using the data gathered from the testing, the designers must decide whether the solution is good enough to meet the client and end user needs and wants by assessment based on the criteria and constraints. Here, the designers must justify or reject design decisions based on the background research gathered while learning about the problem and on the evidence gathered during the testing of the solution. The designers must now decide whether to present the current solution to the client as a possibility or to do more iterations of design on the solution. If they decide that improvements need to be made to the solution, the designers must decide if there is more that needs to be understood about the problem, client, or end user; if another design idea should be tried; or if more planning needs to be conducted on the same design. One way or another, more work needs to be done.

Throughout the process of designing a solution to meet a client's needs and wants, designers work in teams and must communicate to each other, the client, and likely the end user. Teamwork is important in engineering design because multiple perspectives and differing skills and knowledge are valuable when working to solve problems. Communication is key to the success of the designed solution. Designers must communicate their ideas clearly using many different representations, such as text in an engineering notebook, diagrams, flowcharts, technical briefs, or memos to the client.

LEARNING CYCLE

The same format for the learning cycle is used in all grade levels throughout the STEM Road Map, so that students engage in a variety of activities to learn about phenomena in the modules thoroughly and have consistent experiences in the problem- and project- based learning modules. Expectations for learning by younger students are not as high as for older students, but the format of the progression of learning is the same. Students who have learned with curriculum from the STEM Road Map in early

grades know what to expect in later grades. The learning cycle consists of five parts – Introductory Activity/Engagement, Activity/Exploration, Explanation, Elaboration/ Application of Knowledge, and Evaluation/Assessment – and is based on the empirically tested 5E model from BSCS (Bybee et al., 2006).

In the Introductory Activity/Engagement phase, teachers introduce the module challenge and use a unique approach designed to pique students' curiosity. This phase gets students to start thinking about what they already know about the topic and begin wondering about key ideas. The Introductory Activity/Engagement phase positions students to be confident about what they are about to learn, because they have prior knowledge, and clues them into what they don't yet know.

In the Activity/Exploration phase, the teacher sets up activities in which students experience a deeper look at the topics that were introduced earlier. Students engage in the activities and generate new questions or consider possibilities using preliminary investigations. Students work independently, in small groups, and in whole-group settings to conduct investigations, resulting in common experiences about the topic and skills involved in the real-world activities. Teachers can assess students' development of concepts and skills based on the common experiences during this phase.

During the Explanation phase, teachers direct students' attention to concepts they need to understand and skills they need to possess to accomplish the challenge. Students participate in activities to demonstrate their knowledge and skills to this point, and teachers can pinpoint gaps in student knowledge during this phase.

In the Elaboration/Application of Knowledge phase, teachers present students with activities that engage in higher-order thinking to create depth and breadth of student knowledge, while connecting ideas across topics within and across STEM. Students apply what they have learned thus far in the module to a new context or elaborate on what they have learned about the topic to a deeper level of detail.

In the last phase, Evaluation/Assessment, teachers give students summative feedback on their knowledge and skills as demonstrated through the challenge. This is not the only point of assessment (as discussed in the section on Embedded Formative Assessments), but it is an assessment of the culmination of the knowledge and skills for the module. Students demonstrate their cognitive growth at this point and reflect on how far they have come since the beginning of the module. The challenges are designed to be multidimensional in the ways students must collaborate and communicate their new knowledge.

STEM RESEARCH NOTEBOOK

One of the main components of the *STEM Road Map Curriculum Series* is the STEM Research Notebook, a place for students to capture their ideas, questions, observations, reflections, evidence of progress, and other items associated with their daily work. At the beginning of each module, the teacher walks students through the setup of the STEM Research Notebook, which could be a three-ring binder, composition book, or spiral notebook. You may wish to have students create divided sections so that they can easily access work from various disciplines during the module. Electronic notebooks kept on student devices are also acceptable and encouraged. Students will develop their own table of contents and create chapters in the notebook for each module.

Each lesson in the *STEM Road Map Curriculum Series* includes one or more prompts that are designed for inclusion in the STEM Research Notebook and appear as questions or statements that the teacher assigns to students. These prompts require students to apply what they have learned across the lesson to solve the big problem or challenge for that module. Each lesson is designed to meaningfully refer students to the larger problem or challenge they have been assigned to solve with their teams. The STEM Research Notebook is designed to be a key formative assessment tool, as students' daily entries provide evidence of what they are learning. The notebook can be used as a mechanism for dialogue between the teacher and students, as well as for peer and self-evaluation.

The use of the STEM Research Notebook is designed to scaffold student notebooking skills across the grade bands in the *STEM Road Map Curriculum Series*. In the early grades, children learn how to organize their daily work in the notebook as a way to collect their products for future reference. In elementary school, students structure their notebooks to integrate background research along with their daily work and lesson prompts. In the upper grades (middle and high school), students expand their use of research and data gathering through team discussions to more closely mirror the work of STEM experts in the real world.

THE ROLE OF ASSESSMENT IN THE *STEM ROAD MAP CURRICULUM SERIES*

Starting in the middle years and continuing into secondary education, the word *assessment* typically brings grades to mind. These grades may take the form of a letter or a percentage, but they typically are used as a representation of a student's content mastery. If well thought out and implemented, however, classroom assessment can offer teachers, parents, and students valuable information about student learning and misconceptions that does not necessarily come in the form of a grade (Popham, 2013).

The *STEM Road Map Curriculum Series* provides a set of assessments for each module. Teachers are encouraged to use assessment information for more than just assigning grades to students. Instead, assessments of activities requiring students to actively engage in their learning, such as student journaling in STEM Research Notebooks, collaborative presentations, and constructing graphic organizers, should be used to move student learning forward. Whereas other curriculum with assessments may include objective-type (multiple-choice or matching) tests, quizzes, or worksheets, we have

intentionally avoided these forms of assessments to better align assessment strategies with teacher instruction and student learning techniques. Since the focus of this book is on project- or problem-based STEM curriculum and instruction that focuses on higher-level thinking skills, appropriate and authentic performance assessments were developed to elicit the most reliable and valid indication of growth in student abilities (Brookhart & Nitko, 2008).

Comprehensive Assessment System

Assessment throughout all STEM Road Map curriculum modules acts as a comprehensive system in which formative and summative assessments work together to provide teachers with high-quality information on student learning. Formative assessment occurs when the teacher finds out formally or informally what a student knows about a smaller, defined concept or skill and provides timely feedback to the student about his or her level of proficiency. Summative assessments occur when students have performed all activities in the module and are given a cumulative performance evaluation in which they demonstrate their growth in learning.

A comprehensive assessment system can be thought of as akin to a sporting event. Formative assessments are the practices: It is important to accomplish them consistently, they provide feedback to help students improve their learning, and making mistakes can be worthwhile if students are given an opportunity to learn from them. Summative assessments are the competitions: Students need to be prepared to perform at the best of their ability. Without multiple opportunities to practice skills along the way through formative assessments, students will not have the best chance of demonstrating growth in abilities through summative assessments (Black & Wiliam, 1998).

Embedded Formative Assessments

Formative assessments in this module serve two main purposes: to provide feedback to students about their learning and to provide important information for the teacher to inform immediate instructional needs. Providing feedback to students is particularly important when conducting problem- or project-based learning because students take on much of the responsibility for learning, and teachers must facilitate student learning in an informed way. For example, if students are required to conduct research for the Activity/Exploration phase but are not familiar with what constitutes a reliable resource, they may develop misconceptions based on poor information. When a teacher monitors this learning through formative assessments and provides specific feedback related to the instructional goals, students are less likely to develop incomplete or incorrect conceptions in their independent investigations. By using formative assessment to detect problems in student learning and then acting on this information, teachers help move student learning forward through these teachable moments.

Formative assessments come in a variety of formats. They can be informal, such as asking students probing questions related to student knowledge or tasks or simply observing students engaged in an activity to gather information about student skills. Formative assessments can also be formal, such as a written quiz or a laboratory practical. Regardless of the type, three key steps must be completed when using formative assessments (Sondergeld et al., 2010). First, the assessment is delivered to students so that teachers can collect data. Next, teachers analyze the data (student responses) to determine student strengths and areas that need additional support. Finally, teachers use the results from information collected to modify lessons and create learning environments that reinforce weak points in student learning. If student learning information is not used to modify instruction, the assessment cannot be considered formative in nature. Formative assessments can be about content, science process skills, or even learning skills. When a formative assessment focuses on content, it assesses student knowledge about the disciplinary core ideas from the *Next Generation Science Standards* (*NGSS*) or content objectives from *Common Core State Standards for Mathematics* (*CCSS Mathematics*) or *Common Core State Standards for English Language Arts* (*CCSS ELA*). Content-focused formative assessments ask students questions about declarative knowledge regarding the concepts they have been learning. Process skills formative assessments examine the extent to which a student can perform science and engineering practices from the *NGSS* or process objectives from *CCSS Mathematics* or *CCSS ELA*, such as constructing an argument. Learning skills can also be assessed formatively by asking students to reflect on the ways they learn best during a module and identify ways they could have learned more.

Assessment Maps

Assessment maps or blueprints can be used to ensure alignment between classroom instruction and assessment. If what students are learning in the classroom is not the same as the content on which they are assessed, the resultant judgment made on student learning will be invalid (Brookhart & Nitko, 2008). Therefore, the issue of instruction and assessment alignment is critical. The assessment map for this book (found in Chapter 3) indicates by lesson whether the assessment should be completed as a group or on an individual basis, identifies the assessment as formative or summative in nature, and aligns the assessment with its corresponding learning objectives.

Note that the module includes far more formative assessments than summative assessments. This is done intentionally to provide students with multiple opportunities to practice their learning of new skills before completing a summative assessment. Note also that formative assessments are used to collect information on only one or two learning objectives at a time so that potential relearning or instructional modifications can focus on smaller and more manageable chunks of information. Conversely, summative assessments in the module cover many more learning objectives, as they are traditionally used as final markers of student learning. This is not to say that information collected from summative assessments cannot or should not be used formatively. If teachers find that gaps in student learning persist after a summative assessment is completed, it is important to revisit these existing misconceptions or areas of weakness before moving on (Black et al. 2003).

SELF-REGULATED LEARNING THEORY IN THE STEM ROAD MAP MODULES

Many learning theories are compatible with the STEM Road Map modules, such as constructivism, situated cognition, and meaningful learning. However, we feel that the self-regulated learning theory (SRL) aligns most appropriately (Zimmerman, 2000). SRL requires students to understand that thinking needs to be motivated and managed (Ritchhart et al., 2011). The STEM Road Map modules are student centered and are designed to provide students with choices, concrete hands-on experiences, and opportunities to see and make connections, especially across subjects (Eliason & Jenkins, 2012; NAEYC, 2016). Additionally, SRL is compatible with the modules because it fosters a learning environment that supports students' motivation, enables students to become aware of their own learning strategies, and requires reflection on learning while experiencing the module (Peters & Kitsantas, 2010).

Figure 2.2 SRL Theory

Source: Adapted from Zimmerman (2000).

The theory behind SRL (see Figure 2.2) explains the different processes that students engage in before, during, and after a learning task. Because SRL is a cyclical learning process, the accomplishment of one cycle develops strategies for the next learning cycle. This cyclic way of learning aligns with the various sections in the STEM Road

Map lesson plans on Introductory Activity/Engagement, Activity/Exploration, Explanation, Elaboration/Application of Knowledge, and Evaluation/Assessment. Since the students engaged in a module take on much of the responsibility for learning, this theory also provides guidance for teachers to keep students on the right track.

The remainder of this section explains how SRL theory is embedded within the five sections of each module and points out ways to support students in becoming independent learners of STEM while productively functioning in collaborative teams.

Before Learning: Setting the Stage

Before attempting a learning task such as the STEM Road Map modules, teachers should develop an understanding of their students' level of comfort with the process of accomplishing the learning and determine what they already know about the topic. When students are comfortable with attempting a learning task, they tend to take more risks in learning and as a result achieve deeper learning (Bandura, 1986).

The STEM Road Map curriculum modules are designed to foster excitement from the very beginning. Each module has an Introductory Activity/Engagement section that introduces the overall topic from a unique and exciting perspective, engaging the students to learn more so that they can accomplish the challenge. The Introductory Activity also has a design component that helps teachers assess what students already know about the topic of the module. In addition to the deliberate designs in the lesson plans to support SRL, teachers can support a high level of student comfort with the learning challenge by finding out if students have ever accomplished the same kind of task and, if so, asking them to share what worked well for them.

During Learning: Staying the Course

Some students fear inquiry learning because they aren't sure what to do to be successful (Peters, 2010). However, the STEM Road Map curriculum modules are embedded with tools to help students pay attention to knowledge and skills that are important for the learning task and to check student understanding along the way. One of the most important processes for learning is the ability for learners to monitor their own progress while performing a learning task (Peters, 2012). The modules allow students to monitor their progress with tools such as the STEM Research Notebooks, in which they record what they know and can check whether they have acquired a complete set of knowledge and skills. The STEM Road Map modules support inquiry strategies that include previewing, questioning, predicting, clarifying, observing, discussing, and journaling (Morrison & Milner, 2014). Through the use of technology throughout the modules, inquiry is supported by providing students access to resources and data while enabling them to process information, report the findings, collaborate, and develop 21st century skills.

It is important for teachers to encourage students to have an open mind about alternative solutions and procedures (Milner & Sondergeld, 2015) when working through the STEM Road Map curriculum modules. Novice learners can have difficulty knowing what to pay attention to and tend to treat each possible avenue for information as equal (Benner, 1984). Teachers are the mentors in a classroom and can point out ways for students to approach learning during the Activity/Exploration, Explanation, and Elaboration/Application of Knowledge portions of the lesson plans to ensure that students pay attention to the important concepts and skills throughout the module. For example, if a student is to demonstrate conceptual awareness of motion when working on roller coaster research, but the student has misconceptions about motion, the teacher can step in and redirect student learning.

After Learning: Knowing What Works

The classroom is a busy place, and it may often seem that there is no time for self-reflection on learning. Although skipping this reflective process may save time in the short term, it reduces the ability to take into account things that worked well and things that didn't so that teaching the module may be improved next time. In the long run, SRL skills are critical for students to become independent learners who can adapt to new situations. By investing the time it takes to teach students SRL skills, teachers can save time later, because students will be able to apply methods and approaches for learning that they have found effective to new situations. In the Evaluation/Assessment portion of the STEM Road Map curriculum modules, as well as in the formative assessments throughout the modules, two processes in the after-learning phase are supported: evaluating one's own performance and accounting for ways to adapt tactics that didn't work well. Students have many opportunities to self-assess in formative assessments, both in groups and individually, using the rubrics provided in the modules.

The designs of the *NGSS* and *CCSS* allow for students to learn in diverse ways, and the STEM Road Map curriculum modules emphasize that students can use a variety of tactics to complete the learning process. For example, students can use STEM Research Notebooks to record what they have learned during the various research activities. Notebook entries might include putting objectives in students' own words, compiling their prior learning on the topic, documenting new learning, providing proof of what they learned, and reflecting on what they felt successful doing and what they felt they still needed to work on. Perhaps students didn't realize that they were supposed to connect what they already knew with what they learned. They could record this and would be prepared in the next learning task to begin connecting prior learning with new learning.

SAFETY IN STEM

Student safety is a primary consideration in all subjects but is an area of particular concern in science, where students may interact with unfamiliar tools and materials that may pose additional safety risks. It is important to implement safety practices within the context of STEM investigations, whether in a classroom laboratory or in the field. When you keep safety in mind as a teacher, you avoid many potential issues with the lesson while also protecting your students.

STEM safety practices encompass things considered in the typical science classroom. Ensure that students are familiar with basic safety considerations, such as wearing protective equipment (e.g., safety glasses or goggles and latex-free gloves) and taking care with sharp objects, and know emergency exit procedures. Teachers should learn beforehand the locations of the safety eyewash, fume hood, fire extinguishers, and emergency shut-off switch in the classroom and how to use them. Also be aware of any school or district safety policies that are in place and apply those that align with the work being conducted in the lesson. It is important to review all safety procedures annually.

STEM investigations should always be supervised. Each lesson in the modules includes teacher guidelines for applicable safety procedures that should be followed. Before each investigation, teachers should go over these safety procedures with the student teams. Some STEM focus areas such as engineering require that students can demonstrate how to properly use equipment in the maker space before the teacher allows them to proceed with the lesson.

Information about classroom science safety, including a safety checklist for science classrooms, general lab safety recommendations, and links to other science safety resources, is available at the Council of State Science Supervisors (CSSS) website at *www.cosss.org/Safety-Resources*. The National Science Teachers Association (NSTA) provides a list of science rules and regulations, including standard operating procedures for lab safety, and a safety acknowledgement form for students and parents or guardians to sign. You can access these resources at *http://static.nsta.org/pdfs/SafetyIn-TheScienceClassroom.pdf*. In addition, NSTA's Safety in the Science Classroom web page (*www.nsta.org/safety*) has numerous links to safety resources, including papers written by the NSTA Safety Advisory Board.

Disclaimer: The safety precautions for each activity are based on use of the recommended materials and instructions, legal safety standards, and better professional practices. Using alternative materials or procedures for these activities may jeopardize the level of safety and therefore is at the user's own risk.

REFERENCES

Bandura, A. (1986). *Social foundations of thought and action: A social cognitive theory*. Prentice-Hall.

Barell, J. (2006). *Problem-based learning: An inquiry approach*. Corwin Press.

Benner, P. (1984). *From novice to expert: Excellence and power in clinical nursing practice*. Addison-Wesley Publishing Company.

Black, P., Harrison, C., Lee, C., Marshall, B., & Wiliam, D. (2003). *Assessment for learning: Putting it into practice*. Open University Press.

Black, P., & Wiliam, D. (1998). Inside the black box: Raising standards through classroom assessment. *Phi Delta Kappan*, *80*(2), 139–148.

Blumenfeld, P., Soloway, E., Marx, R., Krajcik, J., Guzdial, M., & Palincsar, A. (1991). Motivating project-based learning: Sustaining the doing, supporting learning. *Educational Psychologist*, *26*(3), 369–398.

Brookhart, S. M., & Nitko, A. J. (2008). *Assessment and grading in classrooms*. Pearson.

Bybee, R., Taylor, J., Gardner, A., Scotter, P., Carlson, J., Westbrook, A., & Landes, N. (2006). *The BSCS 5E instructional model: Origins and effectiveness*.

Eliason, C. F., & Jenkins, L. T. (2012). *A practical guide to early childhood curriculum* (9th ed.). Merrill.

Johnson, C. (2003). Bioterrorism is real-world science: Inquiry-based simulation mirrors real life. *Science Scope*, *27*(3), 19–23.

Krajcik, J., & Blumenfeld, P. (2006). Project-based learning. In R. K. Sawyer (Ed.), *The Cambridge handbook of the learning sciences* (pp. 317–334). Cambridge University Press.

Lambros, A. (2004). *Problem-based learning in middle and high school classrooms: A teacher's guide to implementation*. Corwin Press.

Milner, A. R., & Sondergeld, T. (2015). Gifted urban middle school students: The inquiry continuum and the nature of science. *National Journal of Urban Education and Practice*, *8*(3), 442–461.

Morrison, V., & Milner, A. R. (2014). Literacy in support of science: A closer look at cross-curricular instructional practice. *Michigan Reading Journal*, *46*(2), 42–56.

National Association for the Education of Young Children (NAEYC). (2016). Developmentally appropriate practice position statements. *www.naeyc.org/positionstatements/dap*.

Peters, E. E. (2010). Shifting to a student-centered science classroom: An exploration of teacher and student changes in perceptions and practices. *Journal of Science Teacher Education*, *21*(3), 329–349.

Peters, E. E. (2012). Developing content knowledge in students through explicit teaching of the nature of science: Influences of goal setting and self-monitoring. *Science and Education*, *21*(6), 881–898.

Peters, E. E., & Kitsantas, A. (2010). The effect of nature of science metacognitive prompts on science students' content and nature of science knowledge, metacognition, and self-regulatory efficacy. *School Science and Mathematics*, *110*(8), 382–396.

Popham, W. J. (2013). *Classroom assessment: What teachers need to know* (7th ed.). Pearson.

Ritchhart, R., Church, M., & Morrison, K. (2011). *Making thinking visible: How to promote engagement, understanding, and independence for all learners*. Jossey-Bass.

Sondergeld, T. A., Bell, C. A., & Leusner, D. M. (2010). Understanding how teachers engage in formative assessment. *Teaching and Learning*, *24*(2), 72–86.

Zimmerman, B. J. (2000). Attaining self-regulation: A social-cognitive perspective. In M. Boekaerts, P. Pintrich, & M. Zeidner (Eds.), *Handbook of self-regulation* (pp. 13–39). Academic Press.

PART 2

GLOBAL POPULATION ISSUES

STEM ROAD MAP MODULE

GLOBAL POPULATION ISSUES MODULE OVERVIEW

Adrienne Redmond-Sanogo, Juliana Utley, Toni A. Ivey, Sue Christian Parsons, Janet B. Walton, Carla C. Johnson, and Erin E. Peters-Burton

MODULE SUMMARY

In this module, students will explore global population issues through scientific and mathematical lenses as they consider population density with a focus on agriculture. In agriculture, it is often difficult to conduct an exact count of livestock due to the size of the area that the animals inhabit. Similarly, obtaining an accurate count of animals in the wild is a challenge. Population density refers to the application of mathematical modeling to measure a given population within a targeted area or region. In this module, student teams will work to devise models for counting populations of a given species on Earth and develop a formal presentation of their models for consideration by a panel of experts (adapted from Johnson et al., 2015).

The formal presentation will be multifaceted, giving students the opportunity to share their expertise in population density modeling for their given species. Students will examine species' ecosystems, explore global populations through an economic and geographical lens, take on the role of urban planners as they develop megacities that apply their learning about the consequences of population density and overpopulation, and apply species population density models (adapted from Johnson et al., 2015).

ESTABLISHED GOALS AND OBJECTIVES

By the end of this module, students will be able to do the following:

- Explain how to gather information about a population and make valid generalizations and inferences from this information

- Use mathematical practices to complete mathematical explorations related to population size and population density

- Explain the impact of population density on humans and the environment

- Explain the influence of population density on humans and the environment through various forms of writing and speaking

- Identify and explain historical, social, geographical, and economic factors related to population density

CHALLENGE OR PROBLEM FOR STUDENTS TO SOLVE: POPULATION MODELING CHALLENGE

Students will answer the following question in the module's culminating challenge: What is an appropriate mathematical model to measure the population of an identified species on Earth? In this challenge, student teams will devise a model for counting populations of species on Earth. Student teams will each become experts in a species assigned to them, and will work to understand the species' ecosystem and the species' impact on the global ecosystem. Teams will develop a formal presentation of the model for consideration by a panel of experts.

CONTENT STANDARDS ADDRESSED IN THIS STEM ROAD MAP MODULE

A full listing with descriptions of the standards this module addresses can be found in the Appendix. Listings of the particular standards addressed within lessons are provided in a table for each lesson in Chapter 4.

STEM RESEARCH NOTEBOOK

Each student should maintain a STEM Research Notebook, which will serve as a place for students to organize their work throughout this module (see pp. 14–15 for more general discussion on setup and use of the notebook). All written work in the module should be included in the notebook, including records of students' thoughts and ideas, fictional accounts based on the concepts in the module, and records of student progress through the engineering design process. The notebooks may be maintained across subject areas, giving students the opportunity to see that although their classes may be separated during the school day, the knowledge they gain is connected. You may also wish to have students include the STEM Research Notebook Guidelines student handout on page 27 in their notebooks.

Emphasize to students the importance of organizing all information in a research notebook. Explain to them that scientists and other researchers maintain detailed research notebooks in their work. These notebooks, which are crucial to researchers' work because they contain critical information and track the researchers' progress, are often considered legal documents for scientists who are pursuing patents or wish to provide proof of their discovery process.

STUDENT HANDOUT

STEM RESEARCH NOTEBOOK GUIDELINES

STEM professionals record their ideas, inventions, experiments, questions, observations, and other work details in notebooks so that they can use these notebooks to help them think about their projects and the problems they are trying to solve. You will each keep a STEM Research Notebook during this module that is like the notebooks that STEM professionals use. In this notebook, you will include all your work and notes about ideas you have. The notebook will help you connect your daily work with the big problem or challenge you are working to solve.

It is important that you organize your notebook entries under the following headings:

1. **Chapter Topic or Title of Problem or Challenge:** You will start a new chapter in your STEM Research Notebook for each new module. This heading is the topic or title of the big problem or challenge that your team is working to solve in this module.

2. **Date and Topic of Lesson Activity for the Day:** Each day, you will begin your daily entry by writing the date and the day's lesson topic at the top of a new page. Write the page number both on the page and in the table of contents.

3. **Information Gathered from Research:** This is information you find from outside resources such as websites or books.

4. **Information Gained from Class or Discussions with Team Members:** This information includes any notes you take in class and notes about things your team discusses. You can include drawings of your ideas here, too.

5. **New Data Collected from Investigations:** This includes data gathered from experiments, investigations, and activities in class.

6. **Documents:** These are handouts and other resources you may receive in class that will help you solve your big problem or challenge. Paste or staple these documents in your STEM Research Notebook for safekeeping and easy access later.

7. **Personal Reflections:** Here, you record your own thoughts and ideas on what you are learning.

8. **Lesson Prompts:** These are questions or statements that your teacher assigns you within each lesson to help you solve your big problem or challenge. You will respond to the prompts in your notebook.

9. **Other Items:** This section includes any other items your teacher gives you or other ideas or questions you may have.

MODULE LAUNCH

Students will start with a five-minute quick write about what they know about the term "population density" or what they think the term means, and why they think it is important. Next, students will share their responses in small groups of three to four students and then via a whole-class discussion. Following this discussion, students will begin to explore population density by watching a video on the topic (for example, the video "Population Density" at Griffiths, A., & Grant, B. (1985). High school students' understanding of food webs: Identification of a learning hierarchy and related misconceptions. *Journal of Research in Science Teaching*, 22(5), 421–436.) and creating a class list of relevant vocabulary words (e.g., population density, sparsely populated, densely populated, high density, low density). Students will then participate in a think-pair-share exercise about what each term means, after which pairs of students share their thoughts on each term.

Next, the class will discuss the module challenge. Students will learn that, working in teams of three to four, they will be assigned a species that lives on Earth and will determine an appropriate mathematical model to measure the population of their identified species.

PREREQUISITE SKILLS FOR THE MODULE

Students enter this module with a wide range of preexisting skills, information, and knowledge. Table 3.1 provides an overview of prerequisite skills and knowledge that students are expected to apply in this module, along with examples of how they apply this knowledge throughout the module. Differentiation strategies are also provided for students who may need additional support in acquiring or applying this knowledge.

Table 3.1 Prerequisite Key Knowledge and Examples of Applications and Differentiation Strategies

Prerequisite Key Knowledge	Application of Knowledge	Differentiation for Students Needing Knowledge
Mathematics		
• Multiply whole numbers. • Understand, calculate, and apply formulas to find the perimeter and area of rectangles and triangles.	• Students will use whole number operations in this module to determine population density sample size. • In order to understand population density, students will need to be able to calculate the area of a rectangle and circle with whole number and fractional side measurements.	• Provide calculators. • Use anchor charts and other representations to help students understand coordinate grids.

3

Table 3.1 (*continued*)

Prerequisite Key Knowledge	Application of Knowledge	Differentiation for Students Needing Knowledge
Mathematics		
• Solve multiplication problems with fractions and mixed numbers. • Solve real-world problems involving division with fractions. • Understand ratio and percent and solve problems involving ratio and percent in real-world contexts. • Solve problems using the four quadrants of the coordinate plane. • Pose statistical questions, collect data, account for variability in the data, and represent data using a variety of representations.	• Students will have to understand ratios and proportions in order to be able to estimate the population of a species. • Students will use percentages and ratio reasoning to estimate their population. • Students will create graphs and interpret graphs throughout the module so it will be important for them to understand how to read and plot points in the four quadrants of a Cartesian plane. • Students will apply area and perimeter in the context of population density. When they are using grid-sampling techniques, it will be vital for them to understand the concept of area and perimeter. • Students will explore sampling and drawing inferences and conclusions during their sampling activity in math.	• Allow students to have access to hundreds grids, physical manipulatives, and other representations so that they can work with fractions and decimals. • Use ratio tables and words to help students understand ratios. • Work with students individually and pair them with other students in order to help them understand statistics and probability. Teachers may need to provide support in the form of questions and guided instruction.
Science		
• Ask questions, make predictions, and plan and conduct investigations. • Represent and organize data into tables, graphs, drawings, or diagrams.	• Students will explore population distribution and density by asking questions, making logical predictions, planning investigations, and recording data. • Students will explore and create graphical representations of their data throughout the unit.	• While students are designing and conducting open-ended scientific investigations, they will be working with a small group of students; pair students strategically if needed to support the learning of others.

Table 3.1 (*continued*)

Prerequisite Key Knowledge	Application of Knowledge	Differentiation for Students Needing Knowledge
Science		
• Understand the engineering design process and using technology to solve problems.	• Students will compare the results of an investigation with what scientists already accept about this question. • Students will maintain a STEM Research Notebook that includes observations, data, diagrams, calculations, and explanations. • Students will identify appropriate materials, tools, and machines that can extend or enhance the ability to solve a specified problem. • Students will apply a creative design strategy to solve a particular problem generated by societal needs and wants (issues related to high population density).	• Provide a graphic organizer or checklist to help guide students who may struggle with conducting open-ended investigations. • Provide a few options of possible tools for students who struggle with choosing the appropriate tools and techniques to gather, organize, analyze, and interpret data; encourage students to use technology to organize, analyze, and interpret their data. • Allow students who struggle with written expression to keep an electronic STEM Research Notebook instead of a paper copy. Students can use speech-to-text applications to write up their findings to help them communicate scientific understanding using descriptions, explanations, and models. • Provide students with an organizational structure to help them review an experimental design to determine possible sources of bias or error, state alternative explanations, and identify questions for further investigation.

Table 3.1 (*continued*)

Prerequisite Key Knowledge	Application of Knowledge	Differentiation for Students Needing Knowledge
Science		
		• Guide classroom discussions about using technology tools to help answer questions by asking facilitating questions and providing examples of how tools have helped solve problems. • Provide examples of engineering design failures that led to innovative products and materials to help students understand the design process. • Provide examples of innovative technologies that are being used to solve problems associated with high population density.
English Language Arts		
• Use text to make inferences about the author's meaning and support conclusions by referring to text. • Utilize texts in a variety of formats to make claims and arguments; understand how to use this information to write arguments to support claims. • Evaluate arguments and claims for validity.	Across this unit, readers are engaging with a wide variety of texts in their content classrooms, including analysis and evaluation of data and argument. ELA integration in this module is designed to provide a supportive context for the learning engagements in the science and mathematics classes. Learners engage in ongoing nonfiction reading, reading content-related texts and learning to analyze them for purpose, structures, and features as well as receiving instruction in comprehension strategies.	• The module employs a collection of resource texts that provide the context for reading and writing mini-lessons and that serve to develop background knowledge on climate change; teachers should be sure to include texts in a range of reading levels. • Nonfiction trade books tend to be rich in visual support (e.g., photographs, illustrations, graphics), features that support text access for readers. Explicit teaching of comprehension strategies as addressed

Adrienne Redmond-Sanogo et al.

Table 3.1 (*continued*)

Prerequisite Key Knowledge	Application of Knowledge	Differentiation for Students Needing Knowledge
English Language Arts		
• Read and comprehend complex literary and informational texts independently and proficiently. • Write effectively for a variety of purposes and for various audiences. • Have experience researching and gathering evidence from a variety of print and digital sources. • Have experience preparing and presenting oral presentations individually and with a group; be able to critique and analyze their peers' presentations using evidence and rhetoric.	• Throughout the unit, learners write for a variety of purposes, including exploring their own background knowledge and growing understandings, taking notes in the process of research and integrating and sharing information recorded in this way, creating and sharing presentations and formal writing pieces, and developing action proposals. Students also actively participating in nonfiction writing, writing routinely and applying developing strategies related to nonfiction writing. • Students will prepare and present multimedia presentations and digital storybooks as part of this module.	in the module supports readers in gaining access to these texts and more. Mentor texts should be short and accessible to demonstrate the skills. • The nonfiction writing workshop is by its nature differentiated, as each writer chooses topics and approaches and receives both instruction in specific strategies and conferencing and support. Writing instruction is specifically geared to provide skill support that will help students succeed in the content area engagements. Mentor texts used in the writing workshop serve as direct models for the multimedia and graphic presentations called for in the content engagements. • Lessons allow for paired or small group discussion prior to sharing with large groups. Teachers should monitor and support learners as they work to express their ideas. • Presentation skills are actively developed and supported by teachers and through collaboration and practice.

POTENTIAL STEM MISCONCEPTIONS

Students enter the classroom with a wide variety of prior knowledge and ideas, so it is important to be alert to misconceptions or inappropriate understandings of foundational knowledge. These misconceptions can be classified as one of several types: "preconceived notions," opinions based on popular beliefs or understandings; "nonscientific beliefs," knowledge students have gained about science from sources outside the scientific community; "conceptual misunderstandings," incorrect conceptual models based on incomplete understanding of concepts; "vernacular misconceptions," misunderstandings of words based on their common use versus their scientific use; and "factual misconceptions," incorrect or imprecise knowledge learned in early life that remains unchallenged (NRC, 1997, p. 28). Misconceptions must be addressed and dismantled in order for students to reconstruct their knowledge, and therefore teachers should be prepared to take the following steps:

- Identify students' misconceptions.

- Provide a forum for students to confront their misconceptions.

- Help students reconstruct and internalize their knowledge, based on scientific models.

(NRC, 1997, p. 29)

Keeley and Harrington (2010) recommend using diagnostic tools such as probes and formative assessment to identify and confront student misconceptions and begin the process of reconstructing student knowledge. Keeley's *Uncovering Student Ideas in Science* series contains probes targeted toward uncovering student misconceptions in a variety of areas and may be useful resources for addressing student misconceptions in this module.

Some commonly held misconceptions specific to lesson content are provided with each lesson so that you can be alert for student misunderstanding of the concepts presented and used during this module.

SELF-REGULATED LEARNING (SRL) PROCESS COMPONENTS

Table 3.2 illustrates some of the activities in the Global Population Issues module and how they align to the SRL processes before, during, and after learning.

INTEGRATING INSTRUCTION ACROSS SUBJECTS IN THE MIDDLE SCHOOL SETTING

The modules of the STEM Road Map take into account that logistics of middle school instruction, such as scheduling and departmentalization, can make teaching integrated subject matter difficult in middle schools. It is not uncommon for the same grade-level

Table 3.2 SRL Learning Process Components

Learning Process Components	Example from Global Population Issues Module	Lesson Number and Learning Component
Before Learning		
Motivates students	Students explore wolves and predator/prey relationships to understand the impact of species populations on ecosystems.	Lesson 1 Activity/Exploration
Evokes prior learning	Students work as a class to create a KWL chart about wolves and predator/prey relationships.	Lesson 1 Activity/Exploration
During Learning		
Focuses on important features	Students examine graphical representations of populations of salmon impacted by sea lice.	Lesson 2 Introductory Activity/Engagement
Helps students monitor their progress	Students use their understanding of sampling strategies to design their own study and reflect on how to apply their prior learning.	Lesson 3 Activity/Exploration
After Learning		
Evaluates learning	Students apply their learning to create their own population counting models and receive feedback on their models and presentations using a rubric.	Lesson 4 Activity/Exploration
Takes account of what worked and what did not work	Students reflect on the feedback they received from their challenge solutions and presentations.	Lesson 4 Elaboration/Application of Knowledge

science and mathematics teachers to have completely different students, which makes integrating science content with content from other subjects difficult. However, we recognize that some schools allow for teachers from different content areas to team teach. The modules of the STEM Road Map Series are written to accommodate both situations – the singular teacher and the teachers who are able to team teach or integrate instruction across subjects in other ways. A teacher who is teaching the module by themselves may choose to follow only the lead subject, offering enrichment activities in the other connecting subjects. Teachers who are teaching the modules in a single subject course may also want to collaborate with their peers in the other disciplinary areas to get ideas for ways to incorporate the supporting connections seamlessly.

Teachers who are able to teach an integrated curriculum can use the module as written for each of the four subjects in the Learning Components sections of the module.

STRATEGIES FOR DIFFERENTIATING INSTRUCTION WITHIN THIS MODULE

For the purposes of this curriculum module, differentiated instruction is conceptualized as a way to tailor instruction – including process, content, and product – to various student needs in your class. A number of differentiation strategies are integrated into lessons across the module. The problem- and project-based learning approaches used in the lessons are designed to address students' multiple intelligences by providing a variety of entry points and methods to investigate the key concepts in the module (for example, investigating population density issues using scientific inquiry, nonfiction literature, journaling, and collaborative design). Differentiation strategies for students needing support in prerequisite knowledge can be found in Table 3.1 (p. 28). You are encouraged to use information gained about student prior knowledge during introductory activities and discussions to inform your instructional differentiation. Strategies incorporated into this lesson include flexible grouping, varied environmental learning contexts, assessments, compacting, tiered assignments and scaffolding, and mentoring.

Flexible Grouping: Students work collaboratively in a variety of activities throughout this module. Grouping strategies you may choose to employ include student-led grouping, placing students in groups according to ability level, grouping students randomly, grouping them so that students in each group have complementary strengths (for instance, one student might be strong in mathematics, another in art, and another in writing), or grouping students according to common interests.

Varied Environmental Learning Contexts: Students have the opportunity to learn in various contexts throughout the module, including alone, in groups, in quiet reading and research-oriented activities, and in active learning in inquiry and design activities. In addition, students learn in a variety of ways through doing inquiry activities, journaling, reading a variety of texts, watching videos, class discussion, and conducting web-based research.

Assessments: Students are assessed in a variety of ways throughout the module, including individual and collaborative formative and summative assessments. Students have the opportunity to produce work via written text, oral and media presentations, and modeling. You may choose to provide students with additional choices of media for their products (for example, PowerPoint presentations, posters, or student-created websites or blogs).

Compacting: Based on student prior knowledge, you may wish to adjust instructional activities for students who exhibit prior mastery of a learning objective.

Because student work in science is largely collaborative throughout the module, this strategy may be most appropriate for mathematics, ELA, or social studies activities. You may wish to compile a classroom database of research resources and supplementary readings for a variety of reading levels and on a variety of topics related to the module's topic to provide opportunities for students to undertake independent reading.

Tiered Assignments and Scaffolding: Based on your awareness of student ability, understanding of concepts, and mastery of skills, you may wish to provide students with variations on activities by adding complexity to assignments or providing more or fewer learning supports for activities throughout the module. For instance, some students may need additional support in identifying key search words and phrases for web-based research or may benefit from cloze sentence handouts to enhance vocabulary understanding. Other students may benefit from expanded reading selections and additional reflective writing or from working with manipulatives and other visual representations of mathematical concepts. You may also work with your school librarian to compile a set of topical resources at a variety of reading levels.

STRATEGIES FOR ENGLISH LANGUAGE LEARNERS

Students who are developing proficiency in English language skills require additional supports to simultaneously learn academic content and the specialized language associated with specific content areas. WIDA has created a framework for providing support to these students and makes available rubrics and guidance on differentiating instructional materials for English language learners (ELLs) (see *www.wida.us*). In particular, ELL students may benefit from additional sensory supports such as images, physical modeling, and graphic representations of module content, as well as interactive support through collaborative work. This module incorporates a variety of sensory supports and offers ongoing opportunities for ELL students to work with collaboratively. The focus on population density and related issues provides an opportunity for ELL students to share culturally diverse experiences with these topics.

Teachers differentiating instruction for ELL students should carefully consider the needs of these students as they introduce and use academic language in various language domains (listening, speaking, reading, and writing) throughout this module. To adequately differentiate instruction for ELL students, teachers should have an understanding of the proficiency level of each student. The following five overarching grades 6–8 WIDA learning standards are relevant to this module:

- Standard 1: Social and Instructional Language. Focus on assignments/research, resources and supplies, social interaction, use of information, and use of multiple resources.

- Standard 2: The language of Language Arts. Focus on editorials, historical documents, technical texts, biographies, and multimedia.

- Standard 3: The language of Mathematics. Focus on algebraic equations, area, data interpretation and statistics, data sets and plots, estimation, measures of central tendency, percent, probability, and ratio and proportion.

- Standard 4: The language of Science. Focus on climate zones; populations, resources, and environments; and scientific tools or instruments.

- Standard 5: The language of Social Studies. Focus on cultural perspectives and frames of reference, human resources, and maps.

SAFETY CONSIDERATIONS FOR THE ACTIVITIES IN THIS MODULE

All laboratory occupants must wear safety glasses or goggles during all phases of inquiry activities (setup, hands-on investigation, and takedown). For more general safety guidelines, see the section on Safety in STEM in Chapter 2 (pp. 20–21) and for lesson-specific safety information, see the Safety Notes section of each lesson in Chapter 4.

Teachers should develop an Internet/blog protocol with students if guidelines are not already in place. Since students will use the Internet to acquire the needed data for their research, teachers should monitor students' access to the Internet to ensure that students are only accessing websites that are clearly identified by the teacher. The teacher should also inform parents/guardians that students will create online multimedia presentations of their research and that these projects will be closely monitored by the teacher. It is recommended that the teacher not allow any website posts created by students to be publicly posted without teacher approval.

DESIRED OUTCOMES AND MONITORING SUCCESS

The desired outcomes for this module are outlined in Table 3.3, along with suggested ways to gather evidence to monitor student success. For more specific details on desired outcomes, see the Established Goals and Objectives sections for the module and individual lessons.

ASSESSMENT PLAN OVERVIEW AND MAP

Table 3.4 provides an overview of the major group and individual *products* and *deliverables*, or things that comprise the assessment for this module. See Table 3.5 for a full assessment map of formative and summative assessments in this module.

Table 3.3 Desired Outcomes and Evidence of Success in Achieving Identified Outcomes

Desired Outcome	Evidence of Success in Achieving Identified Outcome	
	Performance Tasks	Other Measures
Students work in teams to develop a model for counting populations of a given species on Earth and develop a formal presentation of their models for consideration by a panel of experts.	Students will be assessed on the following using rubrics that focus on content and application of skills related to academic content: • Team presentation • Species report • Digital story about genetically modified organisms (GMOs) • Sampling strategies assignment • Science research plan • Population counting models poster and presentation	• Students will maintain a STEM Research Notebook to reflect upon strategies that might work as they design their mathematical model to measure population density of a given species on Earth. • KWL (Know/Wonder/Learned) charts will be used in lessons to ensure that students understand the content.

Table 3.4 Major Products/Deliverables in Lead Disciplines for Groups and Individuals

Lesson	Major Group Products/ Deliverables	Major Individual Products/ Deliverables
1	• US State Data Research • Predator–Prey Simulation Activity • Endangered Species Presentation • Population Density Artifact	STEM Research Notebook entries Letter to a politician
2	• Are GMOs the Answer? digital storytelling • Population Density Issue Posters	STEM Research Notebook entries
3	• Sampling Strategy Posters • Research Plan Presentations	STEM Research Notebook entries
4	• Invasive Species Research Presentation • Population Counting Model Research • Mark-Recapture Sampling Activity • Grid Sampling Activity • Transect Activity • Module Challenge - Population Counting	STEM Research Notebook entries

Table 3.5 Assessment Map for Global Population Issues

Lesson	Assessment	Group/Individual	Formative/Summative	Lesson Objective Assessed
1	STEM Research Notebook *prompt*	Individual	Formative	• Define population distribution. • Explain that population distribution is related to geographical, natural, social, demographic, political, and historical features, including the role that terrain, climate, soil fertility, proximity to water, mineral resources, industry, transportation, and urbanization have played in population distribution. • Make conjectures about the population density of a species.
1	Endangered Species Presentation *rubric*	Group	Formative	• Analyze and interpret data from static maps, interactive dynamic maps, data tables, and infographics to make and test conjectures about the population density of a region.
1	KWL Charts *graphic organizer*	Group	Formative	• Define population distribution. • Explain that population distribution is related to geographical, natural, social, demographic, political, and historical features, including the role that terrain, climate, soil fertility, proximity to water, mineral resources, industry, transportation, and urbanization have played in population distribution.
1	Population Density Artifact *rubric*	Group	Formative	• Determine if a distribution is clumped, random, or nearly even. • Explain that population density is the application of mathematical modeling to measure a given population within a targeted area or region and that it is used to examine human populations around the globe. • Analyze and interpret data from static maps, interactive dynamic maps, data tables, and infographics to make and test conjectures about the population density of a region. • Make conjectures about the population density of a species.

Table 3.5 Assessment Map for Global Population Issues

Lesson	Assessment	Group/ Individual	Formative/ Summative	Lesson Objective Assessed
2	Are GMOs the Answer? Digital Storytelling *rubric*	Group	Formative	• Explore and determine psychological, physical, and environmental impacts of population density on humans and other species. • Understand the role that scientists, technology experts, engineers, and mathematicians play in addressing issues caused by high population density.
2	Population Density Issue Poster *rubric*	Group	Formative	• Analyze and interpret data from static maps, interactive dynamic maps, data tables, and infographics to make and test conjectures about the population density of Earth and use this information to make conjectures about world population density. • Explore and determine psychological, physical, and environmental impacts of population density on humans and other species. • Understand the role that scientists, technology experts, engineers, and mathematicians play in addressing issues caused by high population density.
2	STEM Research Notebook *prompt*	Individual	Formative	• Explain how human population density impacts species.
2	Graphing Activities *performance task*	Group	Formative	• Analyze and interpret data from static maps, interactive dynamic maps, data tables, and infographics to make and test conjectures about the population density of Earth and use this information to make conjectures about world population density. • Determine what percent of Earth's surface is habitable and use that information to calculate how much land is needed to support humans.
3	Sampling Strategy Poster checklist	Group	Formative	• Define sample and understand the difference between population and sample. • Explain the reason for using sampling techniques and offer one or two examples. • Identify how to choose an appropriate sampling technique based on a research question.

Table 3.5 Assessment Map for Global Population Issues

Lesson	Assessment	Group/ Individual	Formative/ Summative	Lesson Objective Assessed
3	Research Plan *checklist*	Group	Summative	• Identify how to choose an appropriate sampling technique based on a research question. • Determine if a sample is representative of the population under investigation. • Make generalizations from a sample and apply those to the population. • Determine when it is and isn't appropriate to make inferences about a set of data.
3	STEM Research Notebook *prompt*	Individual	Formative	• Define sample and understand the difference between population and sample. • Explain the reason for using sampling techniques and offer one or two examples.
4	Invasive Species Research Presentation *rubric*	Group	Formative	• Identify an invasive species and identify population implications for other species associated with the presence of invasive species in an area.
4	Population Counting Models Poster *rubric*	Group	Summative	• Identify and apply common mathematical models for counting populations. • Identify advantages and disadvantages of each model for a variety of species.
4	Module Challenge – Population Counting *rubric*	Group	Summative	• Create a mathematical model that will provide an accurate estimate of the population of a species. • Present information about population density and models to estimate population density.
4	STEM Research Notebook *prompt*	Individual	Formative	• Identify and apply common mathematical models for counting populations. • Identify advantages and disadvantages of each model for a variety of species.

MODULE TIMELINE

Tables 3.6–3.10 (pp. 42–43) provide lesson timelines for each week of the module. The timelines are provided for general guidance only and are based on class times of approximately 45 minutes.

Table 3.6 STEM Road Map Module Schedule Week 1

Day 1	Day 2	Day 3	Day 4	Day 5
Lesson 1 Exploring Population Distribution and Density	*Lesson 1 Exploring Population Distribution and Density*	*Lesson 1 Exploring Population Distribution and Density*	*Lesson 1 Exploring Population Distribution and Density*	*Lesson 2 Impact of Population Density*
Launch the module. Introduce challenge.	Exploring population distribution – Wolves of Yellowstone activity.	Predator–Prey Simulation. Area Measurements activity.	US State Data activity. Population Density research and artifact.	Salmon and sea lice graphing activity. Introduce world population counting and trends.

Table 3.7 STEM Road Map Module Schedule Week 2

Day 6	Day 7	Day 8	Day 9	Day 10
Lesson 2 Impact of Population Density	*Lesson 2 Impact of Population Density*	*Lesson 2 Impact of Population Density*	*Lesson 3 Exploring Sampling and Making Generalizations and Inferences*	*Lesson 3 Exploring Sampling and Making Generalizations and Inferences*
Are GMOs the Answer? Digital storytelling Investigate population infographics,	Population Density Posters.	Population Density Posters Exponential Growth Models.	Introduce Gallup Poll research and sampling.	Introduce population size estimating. Class Data – Fruit and Vegetable Consumption.

Table 3.8 STEM Road Map Module Schedule Week 3

Day 11	Day 12	Day 13	Day 14	Day 15
Lesson 3 Exploring Sampling and Making Generalizations and Inferences	*Lesson 3 Exploring Sampling and Making Generalizations and Inferences*	*Lesson 3 Exploring Sampling and Making Generalizations and Inferences*	*Lesson 3 Exploring Sampling and Making Generalizations and Inferences*	*Lesson 3 Exploring Sampling and Making Generalizations and Inferences*
Class Data – Fruit and Vegetable Consumption graphing.	Sampling Strategy Posters.	Sampling Strategy Posters.	Design Your Own Produce Consumption Study.	Design Your Own Produce Consumption Study.

Table 3.9 STEM Road Map Module Schedule Week 4

Day 16	Day 17	Day 18	Day 19	Day 20
Lesson 3 *Exploring Sampling and Making Generalizations and Inferences*	*Lesson 3* *Exploring Sampling and Making Generalizations and Inferences*	*Lesson 4* *Exploring, Understanding, and Developing Mathematical Models to Estimate Population Totals*	*Lesson 4* *Exploring, Understanding, and Developing Mathematical Models to Estimate Population Totals*	*Lesson 4* *Exploring, Understanding, and Developing Mathematical Models to Estimate Population Totals*
Sampling strategy scenario/ Making inferences from a sample/	Research Plan activity/	Census as a total population counting technique.	Invasive Species Research and Presentations.	Population Counting Model Research – Mark-Recapture activity

Table 3.10 STEM Road Map Module Schedule Week 5

Day 21	Day 22	Day 23	Day 24	Day 25
Lesson 4 *Exploring, Understanding, and Developing Mathematical Models to Estimate Population Totals*	*Lesson 4* *Exploring, Understanding, and Developing Mathematical Models to Estimate Population Totals*	*Lesson 4* *Exploring, Understanding, and Developing Mathematical Models to Estimate Population Totals*	*Lesson 4* *Exploring, Understanding, and Developing Mathematical Models to Estimate Population Totals*	*Lesson 4* *Exploring, Understanding, and Developing Mathematical Models to Estimate Population Totals*
Population Counting Model Research – Grid Sampling	Population Counting Model Research – Transect	Teams work on Module Challenge	Teams work on Module Challenge	Teams work on Module Challenge/Present

RESOURCES

The media specialist can help teachers locate resources for students to view and read about population issues, climate change, and related content. Special educators and reading specialists can help find supplemental sources for students needing extra support in reading and writing. Additional resources may be found online. Community resources for this module may include professionals in ecology, biology, environmental conservation, and mathematics.

REFERENCES

Johnson, C. C., Moore, J. T., Utley, J., Breiner, J., Burton, S. R., Peters-Burton, E. E., Walton, J., & Parton C. L. (2015). The STEM Road Map for grades 6–8. In C. C. Johnson, E. E. Peters-Burton, & T. J. Moore (Eds.), *STEM Road Map: A framework for integrated STEM education* (pp. 96–123). Routledge. *www.routledge.com/products/9781138804234*

Keeley, P., & Harrington, R. (2010). *Uncovering student ideas in physical science, volume 1:45 new force and motion assessment probes.* NSTA Press.

WIDA. (2020). *WIDA English language development standards framework, 2020 edition: Kindergarten–grade 12.* Board of Regents of the University of Wisconsin System. *https://wida.wisc.edu/sites/default/files/resource/WIDA-ELD-Standards-Framework-2020.pdf*

GLOBAL POPULATION ISSUES LESSON PLANS

Adrienne Redmond-Sanogo, Juliana Utley, Toni Ivey, Sue Christian Parsons,
Janet B. Walton, Carla C. Johnson, and Erin E. Peters-Burton

Lesson Plan 1:
Exploring Population Distribution and Density

In this lesson, students will explore population distribution and population density. Students will begin to explore how population density is calculated and they will begin to consider the population density of a species.

ESSENTIAL QUESTIONS

- What is population distribution?

- Why do populations distribute the way they do?

- What does population density look like and feel like?

- How is population density similar to and different from population size?

- How do you calculate population density?

ESTABLISHED GOALS AND OBJECTIVES

At the conclusion of this lesson, students will be able to do the following:

- Define population distribution

- Determine if a distribution is clumped, random, or nearly even

- Explain that population distribution is related to geographical, natural, social, demographic, political, and historical features, including the role that terrain, climate, soil fertility, proximity to water, mineral resources, industry, transportation, and urbanization have played in population distribution

- Explain that population density is the application of mathematical modeling to measure a given population within a targeted area or region and that it is used to examine human populations around the globe.

- Analyze and interpret data from static maps, interactive dynamic maps, data tables, and infographics to make and test conjectures about the population density of a region

- Make conjectures about the population density of a species

TIME REQUIRED

4 days (approximately 45 minutes each day; see Table 3.6, p. 42)

MATERIALS

Required Materials for Lesson 1

- STEM Research Notebooks (1 per student; see p. 27 for STEM Research Notebook student handout)

- Chart paper or whiteboard and markers for class KWL chart

- Chart paper or butcher paper for sample habitat diagrams

- Chart paper or butcher paper and/or cardboard big enough to model a square yard (or enough copies of square feet to make a square yard)

- Tape

- Markers to use on chart paper or butcher paper

- Internet access

- 1″ measuring tiles (1 per group of 2—3 students)

- 12-inch rulers (1 per group of 2–3 students)

- Yard sticks (1 per group of 2–3 students)

- Computer or tablets for student research (1 per 2 students).

SAFETY NOTES

Students should use caution when handling scissors or other pointed objects, as the sharp points and blades can cut or puncture skin.

CONTENT STANDARDS AND KEY VOCABULARY

Table 4.1 lists the content standards from the *Next Generation Science Standards* (*NGSS*), *Common Core State Standards* (*CCSS*), and the Framework for 21st Century Learning that this lesson addresses, and Table 4.2 (p. 50) presents the key vocabulary. Vocabulary terms are provided for both teacher and student use. Teachers may choose to introduce some or all of the terms to students.

Table 4.1 Content Standards Addressed in STEM Road Map Module Lesson 1

NEXT GENERATION SCIENCE STANDARDS

PERFORMANCE OBJECTIVES

- MS-ESS3–4. Construct an argument supported by evidence for how increases in human population and per-capita consumption of natural resources impact Earth's systems.
- MS-LS2-1. Analyze and interpret data to provide evidence for the effects of resource availability on organisms and populations of organisms in an ecosystem.
- MS-LS2-2. Construct an explanation that predicts patterns of interactions among organism across multiple ecosystems.
- MS-LS2–4. Construct an argument supported by empirical evidence that changes to physical or biological components of an ecosystem affect populations.

SCIENCE AND ENGINEERING PRACTICES

Constructing Explanations and Designing Solutions
- Construct an explanation that includes qualitative or quantitative relationships between variables that predict phenomena.

Engaging in Argument from Evidence
- Construct an oral and written argument supported by empirical evidence and scientific reasoning to support or refute an explanation or a model for a phenomenon or a solution to a problem.

Analyzing and Interpreting Data
- Analyze and interpret data to provide evidence for phenomena.

Scientific Knowledge is Based on Empirical Evidence
- Science disciplines share common rules of obtaining and evaluating empirical evidence.

DISCIPLINARY CORE IDEAS

ESS3.C: Human Impacts on Earth Systems
- Typically as human populations and per-capita consumption of natural resources increase, so do the negative impacts on Earth unless the activities and technologies involved are engineered otherwise.

LS2.A: Interdependent Relationships in Ecosystems
- Organisms, and populations of organisms, are dependent on their environmental interactions both with other living things and with nonliving factors.
- In any ecosystem, organisms and populations with similar requirements for food, water, oxygen, or other resources may compete with each other for limited resources, access to which consequently constrains their growth and reproduction.
- Growth of organisms and population increases are limited by access to resources.
- Similarly, predatory interactions may reduce the number of organisms or eliminate whole populations of organisms. Mutually beneficial interactions, in contrast, may become so interdependent that each organism requires the other for survival. Although the species involved in these competitive, predatory, and mutually beneficial interactions vary across ecosystems, the patterns of interactions of organisms with their environments, both living and nonliving, are shared.

LS2.C: Ecosystem Dynamics, Functioning, and Resilience
- Ecosystems are dynamic in nature; their characteristics can vary over time. Disruptions to any physical or biological component of an ecosystem can lead to shifts in all its populations.

Table 4.1 (*continued*)

CROSSCUTTING CONCEPTS

Patterns
* Patterns can be used to identify cause and effect relationships.

Cause and Effect
* Cause and effect relationships may be used to predict phenomena in natural or designed systems.

Influence of Science, Engineering, and Technology on Society and the Natural World
* All human activity draws on natural resources and has both short and long-term consequences, positive as well as negative, for the health of people and the natural environment.

Stability and Change
* Small changes in one part of a system might cause large changes in another part.

Science Addresses Questions About the Natural and Material World
* Scientific knowledge can describe the consequences of actions but does not necessarily prescribe the decisions that society takes.

COMMON CORE STATE STANDARDS FOR MATHEMATICS
MATHEMATICAL PRACTICES
* MP1. Make sense of problems and persevere in solving them.
* MP2. Reason abstractly and quantitatively.
* MP3. Construct viable arguments and critique the reasoning of others.
* MP4. Model with mathematics.
* MP5. Use appropriate tools strategically.
* MP6. Attend to precision.
* MP8. Look for and express regularity in repeated reasoning.

COMMON CORE STATE STANDARDS FOR ENGLISH LANGUAGE ARTS
READING STANDARDS
* RI.7.8. Trace and evaluate the argument and specific claims in a text, assessing whether the reasoning is sound and the evidence is relevant and sufficient to support the claims.
* RI.7.9. Analyze how two or more authors writing about the same topic shape their presentations of key information by emphasizing different evidence or advancing different interpretations of facts.

WRITING STANDARDS
* W.7.1. Write arguments to support claims with clear reasons and relevant evidence.
* W.7.1.a. Introduce claim(s), acknowledge alternate or opposing claims, and organize the reasons and evidence logically.
* W.7.1.b. Support claim(s) with logical reasoning and relevant evidence, using accurate, credible sources and demonstrating an understanding of the topic or text.
* W.7.1.c. Use words, phrases, and clauses to create cohesion and clarify the relationships among claim(s), reasons, and evidence.
* W.7.1.e. Provide a concluding statement or section that follows from and supports the argument presented.
* W.7.2. Write informative/explanatory texts to examine a topic and convey ideas, concepts, and information through the selection, organization, and analysis of relevant content.
* W.7.2.a. Introduce a topic clearly, previewing what is to follow; organize ideas, concepts, and information, using strategies such as definition, classification, comparison/contrast, and cause/effect; include formatting (e.g., headings), graphics (e.g., charts, tables), and multimedia when useful to aiding comprehension.

Table 4.1 (*continued*)

- W.7.2.b. Develop the topic with relevant facts, definitions, concrete details, quotations, or other information and examples.
- W.7.2.d. Use precise language and domain-specific vocabulary to inform about or explain the topic.
- W.7.3.c. Use a variety of transition words, phrases, and clauses to convey sequence and signal shifts from one time frame or setting to another.
- W.7.6. Use technology, including the Internet, to produce and publish writing and link to and cite sources as well as to interact and collaborate with others, including linking to and citing sources.
- W.7.7. Conduct short research projects to answer a question, drawing on several sources and generating additional related, focused questions for further research and investigation.
- W.7.8. Gather relevant information from multiple print and digital sources, using search terms effectively; assess the credibility and accuracy of each source; and quote or paraphrase the data and conclusions of others while avoiding plagiarism and following a standard format for citation.
- W.7.9. Draw evidence from literary or informational texts to support analysis, reflection, and research.

SPEAKING AND LISTENING STANDARDS
- SL.7.1. Engage effectively in a range of collaborative discussions (one-on-one, in groups, and teacher-led) with diverse partners on grade 7 topics, texts, and issues, building on others' ideas and expressing their own clearly.
- SL.7.1.a. Come to discussions prepared, having read or researched material under study; explicitly draw on that preparation by referring to evidence on the topic, text, or issue to probe and reflect on ideas under discussion.
- SL.7.1.b. Follow rules for collegial discussions, track progress toward specific goals and deadlines, and define individual roles as needed.
- SL.7.1.c. Pose questions that elicit elaboration and respond to others' questions and comments with relevant observations and ideas that bring the discussion back on topic as needed.
- SL.7.1.d. Acknowledge new information expressed by others and, when warranted, modify their own views.
- SL.7.3. Delineate a speaker's argument and specific claims, evaluating the soundness of the reasoning and the relevance and sufficiency of the evidence.
- SL.7.4. Present claims and findings, emphasizing salient points in a focused, coherent manner with pertinent descriptions, facts, details, and examples; use appropriate eye contact, adequate volume, and clear pronunciation.
- SL.7.5. Include multimedia components and visual displays in presentations to clarify claims and findings and emphasize salient points.

FRAMEWORK FOR 21ST CENTURY LEARNING
- Global Awareness
- Environmental Literacy
- Civic Literacy
- Creativity and Innovation
- Critical Thinking and Problem Solving
- Communication and Collaboration
- Information Literacy
- Media Literacy
- ICT Literacy

Table 4.2 Key Vocabulary in Lesson 1

Key Vocabulary	Definition
clumped distribution	animals, plants, or other living things are clustered together in such a way that in some areas there are many members and in other areas there are none
densely populated (high density)	Many of an identified species are crowded within an identified area
density	how concentrated something is; ratio of the mass of something to its volume
extirpated	to be eradicated or destroyed
habitat	the natural home of animals, plants, or other living things
nearly uniform distribution	animals, plants, or other living things are evenly arranged within a specified area
population	the total of all species within a specified area
population density	population per unit area (e.g., people per square mile)
population distribution	the arrangement or spread of a species in a specified area
pull factors	features/factors that attract a population to a particular location; for example, a good water or food source
push factors	factors that push a population away from where they are currently living – for example, a forest fire or a lack of a food source is an example of a push factor
random distribution	animals, plants, or other living things are arranged without any apparent pattern within a specified area
sparsely populated (low density)	few of an identified species within an identified area
species	a group of animals, plants, or other living things that all share common characteristics and are classified as alike in some manner (from *www.yourdictionary.com/species*)
trophic cascade	an ecological process caused by increases in or decreases in populations of certain species that impacts other species; for example, when the wolf population in an area decreases, the deer population increases

TEACHER BACKGROUND INFORMATION

This lesson provides an introduction to the challenge for the module and builds background knowledge on population distribution and population density, and how population density can be calculated. This lesson also introduces the nonfiction reading and writing workshop in the ELA connection.

Population Density

Population density is an important concept that spans disciplines, particularly mathematics, science, and social studies. Scientists, technology experts, engineers, and mathematicians use population density for a variety of purposes. For example, biologists use population density to explore reasons for low density such as reduced fertility and reduction of resources. Human population density is specifically important to study because there is a limited amount of habitable landmass on the Earth that can sustain life. Over 70% of the Earth's surface is covered by oceans. Approximately one-third of the remaining surface is desert, in which it is difficult to sustain human life without some human intervention such as pumping water. Mountainous regions are also difficult to live in for extended periods of time.

Growing populations provide challenges to sustaining human life. Engineers, scientists, technology experts, and mathematicians will have to work together to create solutions to the challenge of having more people and less habitable land. Thus, it is essential for students to develop an understanding of population density and different models for demonstrating population density.

An in-depth knowledge of population density is not necessary to teach this unit; however, some background will be helpful. The following websites will provide some important information on population density, population growth, and land mass:

- *www.universetoday.com/65639/what-percentage-of-the-earths-land-surface-is-desert/*

- *www.zo.utexas.edu/courses/THOC/land.html*

- *www.ecofuture.org/pop/rpts/mccluney_maxpop.html*

Engineers are working hard to address the issues that overpopulation will have on our Earth's ability to sustain human life. For example, the National Academy of Engineering described a grand challenge for engineering, "Engineering for the Developing World" (*www.engineeringchallenges.org/cms/7126/7356.aspx*). This challenge draws attention to the need for engineers to address "demands for energy, food, land, water, transportation, materials, waste disposal, earth moving, health care, environmental cleanup, telecommunication, and infrastructure" (NAE, 2015).

As part of students' investigation of the impacts of population density on ecosystems, they will learn about the elimination and reintroduction of wolves in Yellowstone

National Park. You should be familiar with the reasons for and consequences of the elimination of the wolves and the process by which they were reintroduced as well as the ecosystem consequences of the reintroduction. Useful resources include the following:

- The National Park Service, "Wolf Restoration" at *www.nps.gov/yell/learn/nature/ wolf-restoration.htm*

- Yellowstone National Park Trips, "Wolf Introduction Changes Ecosystem in Yellowstone" at *www.yellowstonepark.com/things-to-do/wildlife/wolf-reintroduction- changes-ecosystem/*

- National Geographic, "Wolves of Yellowstone" at https://education. nationalgeographic.org/resource/wolves-yellowstone/

- EPA, "The Role of Wolves as a Keystone Species: Examining the Ecological Effects and Conservation Implications of a Reintroduced Top Predator on the Scavenger Guild, Yellowstone National Park" at *https://cfpub.epa.gov/ncer_ abstracts/index.cfm/fuseaction/display.abstractDetail/abstract_id/6782*

It is important to note that population density issues have important global social and health implications. These issues, including equity, famine, and the issues of place and power, are critical in today's world; however, a thorough treatment of them is beyond the scope of this module. Students are provided the opportunity in Lesson 2 to conduct research regarding issues related to population density with the aim of touching on some of these issues. Teachers are encouraged to incorporate discussions of current events related to global population into module content and to connect this content to social studies content that focuses on these important issues in more depth.

Nonfiction Reading and Writing Workshop

A particularly useful structure to support students in the middle grades in reading and writing nonfiction is providing frequent mini-lessons (see below for a suggested structure) that students apply in their ongoing writing. Some helpful resources are:

- *Writing Workshop: The Essential Guide* by Ralph Fletcher and Joann Portalupi (Heinemann, 2001)

- *Nonfiction Craft Lessons: Teaching Information Writing K-8* by Joann Portalupi and Ralph Fletcher (Stenhouse, 2001)

- *Nonfiction Matters: Reading, Writing, and Research in Grades 3–8* by Stephanie Harvey (Stenhouse, 1998)

Because reading nonfiction requires different skills than reading narrative fiction, it is important to teach readers to recognize nonfiction purposes, structures, and features. The nonfiction reading workshop should include focused mini-lessons on nonfiction-specific strategies, using quality mentor texts (real books, articles, etc.) to illustrate and provide practice. A simple mini-lesson structure might include 1) engagement – a quick introduction to activate prior knowledge and gain interest; 2) direct instruction – modeling, explanation, demonstration; 3) guided application – students try it, you check for understanding; 4) link/connection – draw a direct link to ongoing reading students are doing and remind them to use the strategy in their work.

Specific mini-lessons in the ELA reading and writing workshops can relate to steps and processes in inquiry such as the following: determining important information; summarizing and synthesizing information; posing questions before, during, and after reading; and citing sources.

To prepare for module presentations, you may wish to use a nonfiction writing workshop to explore structures and features of ways to present information using mentor texts. Pay particular attention to how writers select structures that serve their communicative purposes and help to focus their writing and how they employ features such as photographs, graphics, and headings to construct engaging and informative texts.

You may wish to consider a source such as Portalupi and Fletcher's (2001) *Nonfiction Craft Lessons: Information Writing K–8, Mini-lessons.* This resource contains information on topics such as discussing opposing views as a way to strengthen an argument.

COMMON MISCONCEPTIONS

Students will have various types of prior knowledge about the concepts introduced in this lesson. Table 4.3 outlines common misconceptions students may have about the lesson content. Because of the breadth of students' experiences, it is not possible to anticipate every misconception that students may bring as they approach this lesson. Incorrect or inaccurate prior understanding of concepts can influence student learning in the future, however, so it is important to be alert to misconceptions such as those presented in the table.

Table 4.3 Common Misconceptions About the Concepts in Lesson 1

Topic	Student Misconception	Explanation
Ecosystems	Changing the population size of some organisms within an ecosystem will not impact the ecosystem because those organisms are not very important.	The nature of an ecosystem is interdependence of organisms and the environment. All organisms within an ecosystem are important and, while a change in population size of some organisms may not impact all other species in the ecosystem to the same extent, it will impact the ecosystem as a whole.

Table 4.3 (*continued*)

Topic	Student Misconception	Explanation
Food webs and food chains	Food webs are the same as food chains.	A food chain typically represents what a particular animal eats and is a single flow of energy within an ecosystem; food webs represent the interaction of various food chains in an ecosystem and therefore encompass interconnected and complex flows of energy.
Measuring population density	One can measure a population by taking one sample and multiplying by the area in which the organism lives.	Population density can be different in different locations because of factors such as availability of food and shelter. To measure population density more accurately, many samples must be taken from various locations.

PREPARATION FOR LESSON 1

Review the Teacher Background Information provided (pp. 51–53), assemble the materials for the lesson, and preview the video and websites recommended in the Learning Plan Components section that follows. Have your students set up their STEM Research Notebooks (see pp. 26–27 for discussion and student instruction handout).

Using butcher paper or chart paper, prepare four identically sized square-shaped habitat models using dots to represent inhabitants for various population densities and distributions. A sample is provided below.

Select species for student teams to explore during the module. Choose species that live in the community or region. Additionally, choose a variety of large organisms (e.g., deer, bear, etc.), small organisms (e.g., beavers, ants, tadpoles, etc.), and microorganisms (e.g., protozoa in water), as well as tree or plant species.

For the Wolves of Yellowstone activity, be prepared to conduct a "picture walk" through a short, accessible book about Yellowstone such as *Bugling Elk and Sleeping*

Figure 4.1 Sample Population Density Models

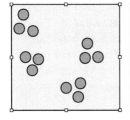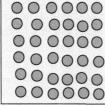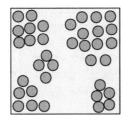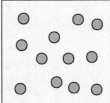

Grizzlies by Shirley Craighead. If you wish to also show a brief video about the park, identify a video such the National Park Service "Experience Yellowstone" video at *www.nps.gov./yell/learn/photosmultimedia/videos.htm*. Be prepared with maps, online mapping resources, and general information about the geography of Yellowstone National Park to draw connections to geography.

For the Predator–Prey Simulation activity, locate an online simulation such as *www. biologycorner.com/worksheets/pred_prey.html* or *http://smithsonianeducation.org/interactives/predatorvsprey/index.html*. Alternatively, prepare an in-class simulation such as that described at *http://serc.carleton.edu/sp/mnstep/activities/26886.html* or *www.wolfquest. org/pdfs/Deer%20Me%20Lesson.pdf*.

Compile a list of US endangered species for students to investigate in the Elaboration/Application of Knowledge section of this lesson. Lists can be found, for example, at U.S. Fish and Wildlife Service, "Endangered Species": *www.fws.gov/program/endangered-species* or Smithsonian Magazine, "North America's Most Endangered Species": *www. smithsonianmag.com/science-nature/north-americas-most-endangered-animals-174367735/*.

Select only species from North America or your home state so that students can best understand how this species interacts with its environment and other species. Include producers, herbivores, and carnivores on the list in order to represent various parts of the food chain.

For mathematics class, be prepared with materials to use to create a model of a square yard (for example, chart paper or butcher paper). Students will suggest how this could be done using materials in the classroom.

Be prepared to assign states to teams of two to three students each in mathematics class; be sure that all states are assigned. Students will research the area and population of each state. For population data, you may wish to have students use the Quick Facts page of the U.S. Census Bureau website at *www.census.gov/quickfacts/fact/table/ US/PST045221* (you may wish to explore this site in advance). Identify the most recent year for which population data is available. Prepare a spreadsheet (using Google Docs or Excel, for example) in which student teams can enter state data.

For the ELA connections in the module, be prepared to help students build background knowledge and to develop skill at reading and writing a variety of nonfiction texts by assembling a wide range of texts related to the topic of population density and ecosystem balance. Most books in this collection should be authentic texts (not constructed just for classroom learning) that are short enough to be read in one or two sittings such as, for example, high-level picture books, booklets and brochures, and articles. Longer nonfiction selections that are structured for exploration rather than reading cover to cover (for example, atlases and guidebooks) are also great resources to have on hand. Keep the collection readily available to students for use in nonfiction reading and writing workshop engagements and provide time each week for students to read and write in their STEM Research Notebooks about what they are learning from their reading.

LEARNING PLAN COMPONENTS
Introductory Activity/Engagement

Connection to the Challenge/Science and Mathematics Classes: Introduce students to the module challenge by having students start with a 5 minute quick write about what they know about the term "population density" or what they think it means and why they think it is important. Have students share their ideas in groups of three to four. As students share, listen to different groups and then sequence a whole-class share.

Next, watch a video on population density such as "Population Density" at *www.youtube.com/watch?v=h5Tpy7MQcf0*. After viewing the video, work as a class to list terms from the video (e.g., population density, sparsely populated, densely populated, high density, low density) and then have students do a think-pair-share about what each term means. Ask pairs of students to share their thoughts on each term with the class.

Tell students they will be keeping a STEM Research Notebook throughout this module. They should record insights from mathematics and their other classes (science, social studies, and language arts) related to population and population density that will help them with their final challenge. Students should then record in their own words in their STEM Research Notebooks the meaning for each of the terms discussed for further reference throughout the module.

Discuss the module challenge. Assign students to teams of three to four. Assign each group a species (see Preparation for Lesson 1, p. 54). Tell students that they will work throughout the module to determine an appropriate mathematical model to measure the population of their teams' species.

Social Studies Connection: Not applicable.

ELA Connection: Not applicable.

Activity/Exploration

Science Class: Students will participate in an exploration of wolves to illustrate the impact of species populations on ecosystems.

Have students each create a KWL (Know/Wonder/Learned) chart in their STEM Research Notebooks. Tell students to silently think about (1) what they KNOW (or think they know) about wolves and record that in the K column of their notes and (2) what they WONDER about wolves and to write that in their STEM Research Notebooks. Give the students a few minutes to record their thoughts.

Create a class KWL chart on chart paper or a whiteboard to aggregate the class responses (note: it is helpful for this chart to be created in a medium where students can revisit it). Have students share their ideas about wolves with the class and record them in the class KWL chart. If the students' responses do not address the issues, ask students to share what they know about where wolves live, what they eat, and what may eat a wolf.

Check for students' understanding of the terms *food webs*, *food chains*, *predator*, and *prey*. If students' understanding of these terms needs to be addressed or refreshed, hold a class discussion about the terms and create definitions that students can enter into their STEM Resarch Notebooks.

Wolves of Yellowstone

Ask the students if they have ever been to a national or state park and have them share their experiences. Ask them if they have ever heard of or been to Yellowstone National Park. For students who have visited Yellowstone, ask them to describe the park. Next, ask students to describe the location of the park. Use maps and online mapping tools to identify the geographical location of the park. Hold a class discussion about the location, geographical and other and natural features of Yellowstone relative to your school's location, geography, and natural features.

Build background knowledge of Yellowstone by reading or doing a "picture walk" through a short, accessible book about Yellowstone such as *Bugling Elk and Sleeping Grizzlies* by Shirley Craighead. You could also view one or more of the brief videos at *www.nps.gov./yell/learn/photosmultimedia/videos.htm.* Emphasize that when Yellowstone became the nation's first national park in 1872, there was an abundance of wolves; however, a century later, there were almost no gray wolves in the park. Ask students to discuss the following questions as a class:

- What do you think happened to the wolf population between 1872 and the mid-1900s?

- What do you think happened when a top predator was removed from the ecosystem?

- What impact does the gray wolf population have on the ecosystem and physical population of Yellowstone National Park?

- Do you think that the wolves have an impact on the rivers that run through Yellowstone? How so?

Show students a video about wolves and their impact on the ecosystem such as one of the following:

- "How Wolves Change Rivers" (www.youtube.com/watch?v=ysa5OBhXz-Q#t=14)

- "Wolves of Yellowstone: EARTH A New Wild" (http://oeta.pbslearningmedia. org/resource/a58e3ca2-52ab-45f5-87ac-26ee0d681146/wolves-of-yellowstone-earth-a-new-wild/)

STEM Research Notebook Prompt

After watching the video, ask students to individually record what they have learned in the L column of the KWL charts they created for wolves in their STEM Research Notebooks. Ask students to create a reflection in their notebooks answering the following questions: What matters here? What matters to you? What matters to people who may have a different perspective than you? What matters to society in general? What is your "take-away?" Would the issues around wolves have an impact on your assigned species? Finally, ask students to write down any new "wonders" about wolves, ecosystems, or other related questions they may have.

Predator–Prey Simulation

Have students work in small groups to simulate predator–prey relationships in ecosystems using an online or classroom game (see Preparation for Lesson 1, pp. 54–55). Have students collect and analyze data, construct graphs, and predict populations for future generations.

Next, introduce the concept of trophic levels in ecosystems as positions in a food chain, sketching a graphic of the levels using a pyramid at which level 1 is at the bottom and level 5 is at the top. At the first level are producers, or plants that make their own food through photosynthesis. The second level are animals that eat plants (herbivores, or primary consumers). The third level is composed of animals that eat herbivores (carnivores, or secondary consumers). The fourth level is animals that eat other carnivores (also secondary consumers). The top level are secondary-consumer predators that have no other predators and are therefore at the top of the food chain.

Next, have students use a computer model to simulate the relationship between three different trophic levels (producers, primary consumers, and secondary consumers) by using the interactive activity (or another similar simulation) found at: *www.shodor.org/interactivate/activities/RabbitsAndWolves/*. Give the students a chance to explore the system by manipulating the variable and to see if they can develop balance in the ecosystem so that all trophic levels survive over time. After students have completed the activity have them create a STEM Research Notebook entry.

STEM Research Notebook Entry

Next, have students create a KWL chart in their STEM Research Notebook for their species. Remind students of the challenge/problem for this module and ask students to write about what they know about where their species lives, what they eat, and what may eat them.

Have student teams conduct research on their assigned species about where the species lives, what they eat, and what eats them. Have students record this information in their STEM Research Notebooks and compare it to the information they recorded above. Then, ask students to answer the following question in their STEM Research Notebooks: What would you need to do to balance the ecosystem of your assigned species so that all trophic levels survive over time?

Mathematics Class: In mathematics class activities, students will explore area measurements as they relate to population distribution and will collect data about the area of and population of US states.

Area Measurements

Display the four identically sized square-shaped habitats you created (see Preparation for Lesson 1, p. 54). Explain to students that the square represents a habitat and the dots represent a species inhabiting the habitat, and remind them that this representation is similar to the video on population density they watched. Ask students the following question:

If all of the habitats are the same size, what do you notice about how the population of the species is distributed within each habitat?

Solicit ideas from the students about the distributions. If students don't notice that some of the species have more space to move about and others don't, ask probing questions such as the following:

- Do you notice any clusters in the distribution?

- Why do you think they are distributed this way?

- Which of these distributions have a clumped distribution? Why?

- Which have a random distribution?

- Which are nearly uniform?

Next, engage the students in a discussion about the size of a square foot, a square yard, and a square mile so that they will be able to understand the relative size of the dimensions. Choose one of the sample habitats and ask:

- The area of this habitat is a square foot. How big is a square foot?

- How could you model a square foot? (i.e., have students work in groups of 2–3 to model a square foot using the one-inch tiles or rulers)

- If the area of this habitat is a square foot, what kind of species would be clustered in this way? How do you know? Are there other species that could cluster this way? Students can refer to species assigned during the launch or other species they are familiar with.

- Using the same habitat, ask students: What if the area of this habitat was one square yard. How big would that actually be?

- How many square feet are in this square yard?

- How could we model this? If students suggest using square tiles, you might say, that may take a lot of time. Is there a more efficient way to model it? Have students suggest ways they could model a square yard; work together as a class to create a model of a square yard using chart paper or butcher paper or other materials in the classroom.

- Next, ask: If the area of this habitat is a square yard, what kind of species would be clustered in this way? How do you know? Are there other species that could cluster this way? We have discussed the size and population distribution for a square foot and a square yard. How big is a square mile? How could we model that?

Have students give you an example of what a square mile would be. Use Google Earth or the Measure Map Lite App if necessary to model what a square mile would be. Ask students the following:

- If the area of this habitat is a square mile, what kind of species would be clustered in this way?

- How do you know?

- Are there other species that could cluster this way?

If students don't bring up humans, suggest it by asking: What if our assigned species were human? Where do you think you would see this population distribution? Ask the same thing about the other distributions.

STEM Research Notebook Entry

Using their STEM Research Notebooks, have students each draw and label, using a diagram similar to the habitat representations you prepared for the class, what they think the population distribution for their assigned species is like. Prompt students to choose the units they will use (square miles, square inches, square feet, etc.) and label their diagrams with the species and the area units used. Have students provide a written explanation of why they chose these units.

US State Data

Assign students to teams of two to three. Provide each team with states to explore, distributing all 50 states among teams, and tell students that they will find the area (in square miles) and population for each state they have been assigned. Discuss with students that they must use credible sources for their data. Have students work as a class to brainstorm ideas about where they might access accurate population data. Show students the U.S. Census Bureau Quick Facts web page (*www.census.gov/quickfacts/*

fact/table/US/PST045221), pointing out the difference between the census estimates and the actual census data available. As a class, discuss why it is important that they be consistent in the year for which they report state populations. Discuss as a class whether students will use the actual census data or the estimates. Ask students: Why is it important to use the data consistently? As a class, agree on a year for which data will be collected.

Have students conduct Internet research to find the population and total land area (in square miles) for each state they have been assigned. Once teams have completed research on their assigned states, have students add that data to a class spreadsheet (see Preparation for Lesson 1, p. 55).

Once all teams have entered their data, ask the students to discuss the following in a whole-class discussion:

- What did you notice about the states you collected data for?

- What are some things that you wonder about the population and land area of their states?

As a class, sort the data in the spreadsheet by population and choose a few states that have similar populations but very different land areas. (For example, Montana and Rhode Island have a similar population but very different land areas.) Choose a few states that have similar population and land area (for example, Kansas and Utah). Hold a class discussion, asking students:

- What do you notice about the population of Montana and Rhode Island?

- What about the land area of each state?

- How big do you think 147,164 square miles would be? Is that bigger or smaller than the state you live in? What about 2,491 square miles?

Point out to students that the two states have similar population but different land areas. Have students think on their own for a minute about how the population may be distributed in these two states and then share their thoughts with a partner. As students discuss with their partners, walk around and monitor students' discussions. Select students to share based on what you notice in their discussions.

Refer to the habitat diagrams you created. Ask students for their ideas about which diagram might best represent each state's population density. Pull up a population density map for both states using a site such as the Statistical Atlas (for example, *https://statisticalatlas.com/state/Rhode-Island/Population* for Rhode Island and *https://statisticalatlas.com/state/Montana/Population* for Montana). Discuss the population densities as a class.

Next, refer to the two states with similar population and land area (for example, Kansas and Utah). Ask students what they notice about Kansas and Utah and whether

they think the population is spread out or clustered close together. Show students the sample of clustered population using the habitat diagrams and compare this to the population density maps.

- What do you notice about the population of Kansas and Utah?

- What about the land area of each state?

Point out to students that Kansas and Utah have similar population and similar land areas. Ask students to think on their own for a minute about how the population may be distributed in these two states and then share their thoughts with a partner. As students discuss with their partner, walk around and monitor students' discussions. Select students to share their ideas with the class based on what you notice in their discussions.

Refer to the habitat diagrams you created. Ask students the following:

- Which of those distributions do you think would be similar to Kansas? Why?

- What about Utah?

Next show population density maps for both states (for example, *https://statisticalatlas.com/state/Kansas/Population* for Kansas and *https://statisticalatlas.com/state/Utah/Population* for Utah). Ask students the following: Why do you think the population is distributed that way?

Next, introduce the idea of metropolitan areas as large cities and the surrounding areas. Ask students: What percentage of the population in the United States do you think lives in metropolitan areas? Have students work in pairs to explore this question on the Internet.

After students have explored this question, bring them back together and have teams share their findings with the class. Display a population density map of the United States, such as the "Where We Live" map found at *www.globalrecruitingroundtable.com/wp-content/uploads/where-we-live-in-us.jpg*.

STEM Research Notebook Entry

Have students examine the population density map of the US and respond to the following prompts:

- How is this map different than other maps we have explored?

- What does this map tell you about the population of the United States?

- What do you think is meant by population density?

- What is a definition of population density?

- Describe what you know about population density in terms of your team's assigned species.

ELA Connection: Launch a nonfiction reading and writing workshop (see Teacher Background Information, pp. 52–53). Over the course of the module, work to strengthen students' abilities to read and understand nonfiction texts and to compose nonfiction texts that are engaging and that effectively convey information.

Use ELA class throughout the module as an opportunity to discuss and add to students' STEM Research Notebooks where students will record their learning and observations related to population density. Discuss with students the role of writing and recording ideas in the inquiry process and the importance of citing the sources of information.

Social Studies Connection: Have students explore the history of national parks in the US, either in teams or individually. You may wish to use a jigsaw approach to student research, assigning each team one or two questions to research and asking teams to report back to the whole class. Specifically, ask students to answer questions such as the following:

- Why were national parks formed?

- How might the ecosystem of a national park area such as Yellowstone be different today if the area had not been preserved as a national park?

- What does the National Park Service's policy on predatory species say should be done about animals in parks that are predators? (this can be found at *www. nps.gov/parkhistory/online_books/anps/anps_2g.htm*)

- Do you think that the National Park Service enforced its rules for predatory animals with wolves?

- What have been the positive effects of reintroducing wolves to Yellowstone (for example, see *https://education.nationalgeographic.org/resource/reintroduction-top-predator*)

- What are some negative effects of reintroducing wolves to Yellowstone? (for example, see *https://extension.colostate.edu/topic-areas/people-predators/public-perspectives-on-wolves-and-wolf-reintroduction-8-004/*)

Hold a class discussion about students' findings and then have each student create a STEM Research Notebook entry.

STEM Research Notebook Entry

Ask students to create an entry in which they reflect on whether the elimination of wolves from Yellowstone aligned with the National Park Service's policy for predatory animals. Then, ask students to answer the following question: Do you believe that the reintroduction of wolves to Yellowstone Park has positive or negative impacts on the ecosystem? Please explain why or why not.

Next, make a deeper connection between human migration and environmental impact by having student investigate how westward expansion in the 1800s impacted

the wolf population in the area that is now Yellowstone National Park. (*www.nps.gov/yell/learn/nature/wolfrest.htm*)

Explanation

Science Class: Have students explain their results from the Predator–Prey Simulation activity. Hold a class discussion on different aspects of ecosystems that play a role in population density (i.e., number of predators, number of prey, rates of reproduction, life longevity, disease, famine, natural disasters).

Discuss the study of ecology: The word *ecology* is derived from the Greek word *oikos*, which means *house*. As such, ecology is the study of where and how organisms live and how they interact with one another and their environment.

Mathematics Class: Access Ben Blatt's *Manifest Destiny* website from Slate.com at *www.slate.com/articles/life/culturebox/2014/10/population_map_use_our_interactive_map_to_figure_out_how_many_flyover_states.html* This site has an *Equal Population Mapper* that allows students to visualize how different parts of the country compare population density. For instance, you can use the map to show how the population of New York City is about the same as Idaho, Montana, Wyoming, North Dakota, South Dakota, Nebraska, and the western half of Minnesota. Have students make and share conjectures about other cities and explore the map as a class.

- How do you think Ben Blatt created this map?

- What information would he need? Teacher note: "The population data come from the 2010 census, and the square mileage was calculated by summing each highlighted county's total area" (Blatt, 2015).

Ask students to explain what population density is. Work as a class to create an accurate definition for population density and have students record the definition in their STEM Research Notebooks. Prompt students with the following questions:

- How is population distribution different from population density?

- How do you think we could calculate the population density of a state such as Montana?

- What does it mean mathematically to calculate the number of people living per unit of area? What if your unit of area is a square mile?

- How would you calculate the population density of the states that you explored earlier in this lesson? Is there more than one way to do this? How could we use technology to calculate the population density?

Next, have students create a STEM Research Notebook entry to connect the discussion to their assigned species.

STEM Research Notebook Entry

Ask students to respond to the following in their STEM Research Notebooks. What do you think the population density is for your assigned species? What information would you need to obtain to calculate that? How could you find that information?

ELA Connection: N.A.

Social Studies Connection: Prompt students to begin to consider migration as a factor in population density changes by engaging students in a discussion on push and pull factors that influence migration. Ask students to discuss the following questions as a class:

- Why do people move from one area to another?

- What are some of the environmental and historical reasons why people have migrated from one area to another?

- What impact does this have on population?

Explain to students that a push factor is something that drives people away from their homes. Ask students if they can think of examples (e.g., war, fires). Ask students if they can think of something that might pull people to a new home (e.g., new opportunities, better weather). Next, have students create a STEM Research Notebook entry connecting these ideas to their assigned species.

STEM Research Notebook Entry

Have students respond to the following question in their STEM Research Notebooks: Are there push and pull factors that might influence the species you are assigned? What would those be?

Elaboration/Application of Knowledge

Science Class: Have students work in pairs. Each pair should select a species on the endangered species list you prepared (see Preparation for Lesson 1, p. 55).

Student pairs should research their assigned species and develop a multimedia presentation that includes the species' habitat, energy sources, predators, etc. Students should research (a) the causes that have led the species to be on the endangered species list, (b) the consequences if the species were to become extinct, (c) how human activity threatens the species' survival, and (d) how humans are helping the species.

Mathematics Class: Have each student create a brochure, website, multimedia presentation, or other artifact that demonstrates their understanding of population distribution and density. Tell students to end their product with their response to the following question: What is the impact of population density on you and your environment?

ELA and Social Studies Connections: Have students compose a letter to a politician requesting support for protecting an endangered species.

Evaluation/Assessment

Students may be assessed on the following performance tasks and other measures listed.

Performance Tasks

- US State Data research
- Predator–Prey Simulation activity
- Endangered Species presentation (rubric)
- Population Density artifact (rubric)
- Letter to Politician

Other Measures

- STEM Research Notebook entries
- Participation in class discussions

Rubric for Performance Assessment Presentations and Artifacts

	Below Mastery	Approaching Mastery	At Mastery
Demonstrated understanding of subject	Student's presentation or artifact does not provide the audience with enough detail to understand the subject, or details provided are inaccurate.	Student's presentation or artifact provides the audience with some detail that demonstrates their understanding of the subject; however, the detail is not sufficient.	Student's presentation or artifact provides the audience with sufficient detail to demonstrate their understanding of the subject. The student used relevant examples to support their statements.
Comments:			
Organization of presentation or artifact	The student's project does not include all of the required components. The organization and order does not make sense or lacks a seamless flow. The main idea is not present or is not clearly stated. The student does not include an introduction or conclusion.	The student's project includes most of the required components. The organization and order moves from one topic to the next, but the topics are not related. The main idea is present but it is not clearly stated.	The student's project includes all of the required components. The organization and order of the presentation follows an effective, logical, and seamless order. The main idea is clearly stated in the presentation.

	Below Mastery	Approaching Mastery	At Mastery
	The student does not use presentation time guidelines effectively. (Too short or too long.)	The student included an introduction and conclusion but they do not clearly introduce the topic and bring it all together in the conclusion. The student met the time requirements but spent too much time on unrelated topics or rushed through important ideas.	The introduction and conclusion were well formulated and effectively introduce and close the presentation. The student met the time requirements. No section of the presentation was rushed. Important points were emphasized.
Comments:			
Use of multimedia/ graphics	The project does not include multimedia and/ or graphics or used media but in a way that distracted from the presentation.	The project includes multimedia and/or graphics but it does not add to the presentation.	The project included multimedia and/or graphics which were used to emphasize important points and add to the interest of the presentation.
Comments:			
Interaction with the audience (for presentations)	Did not respond to the audience's questions and feedback. They were unprepared to answer questions.	Were able to answer some of the audience's questions but not most. If students didn't know an answer they stated that they didn't know or tried to make up an answer.	Responded to audience's questions and feedback. When students didn't understand an audience member's question, they asked for clarification. If the student didn't know the answer to a question, they admitted that they did not know the answer and explained how they would find the answer.
Comments:			
Team participation	Not all team members participated.	All team members participated in the presentation, but not equally.	It is clear that all students participated in the development and presentation of the project.
Comments:			

Adrienne Redmond-Sanogo et al.

INTERNET RESOURCES

Colorado State University Extension, "Public Perspectives on Wolves and Wolf Reintroduction"

- *https://extension.colostate.edu/topic-areas/people-predators/public-perspectives-on-wolves-and-wolf-reintroduction-8-004/*

Endangered species lists

- *www.fws.gov/program/endangered-species*

- *www.smithsonianmag.com/science-nature/north-americas-most-endangered-animals-174367735/*

EPA, "The Role of Wolves as a Keystone Species: Examining the Ecological Effects and Conservation Implications of a Reintroduced Top Predator on the Scavenger Guild, Yellowstone National Park"

- *https://cfpub.epa.gov/ncer_abstracts/index.cfm/fuseaction/display.abstractDetail/abstract_id/6782*

"How Wolves Change Rivers"

- *www.youtube.com/watch?v=ysa5OBhXz-Q#t=14*

National Academy of Engineering, "Engineering for the Developing World"

- *www.engineeringchallenges.org/cms/7126/7356.aspx*

National Geographic, "Reintroduction of the Top Predator"

- *https://education.nationalgeographic.org/resource/reintroduction-top-predator*

National Geographic "Wolves of Yellowstone"

- *www.yellowstonepark.com/things-to-do/wildlife/wolf-reintroduction-changes-ecosystem/*

National Park Service, "Experience Yellowstone"

- *www.nps.gov./yell/learn/photosmultimedia/videos.htm*

National Park Service, policy on predatory species

- *www.nps.gov/parkhistory/online_books/anps/anps_2g.htm*

National Park Service "Wolf Restoration"

- *www.nps.gov/yell/learn/nature/wolf-restoration.htm*

"Population Density"

- *www.youtube.com/watch?v=h5Tpy7MQcf0*

Population density maps

- *https://statisticalatlas.com/state/Kansas/Population*

- *https://statisticalatlas.com/state/Montana/Population*

- *https://statisticalatlas.com/state/Rhode-Island/Population*

- *https://statisticalatlas.com/state/Utah/Population*

Predator–prey simulations

- *www.biologycorner.com/worksheets/pred_prey.html*

- *http://smithsonianeducation.org/interactives/predatorvsprey/index.html*

- *http://serc.carleton.edu/sp/mnstep/activities/26886.html*

- *www.wolfquest.org/pdfs/Deer%20Me%20Lesson.pdf*

Resources for population density, population growth, and land mass

- *www.universetoday.com/65639/what-percentage-of-the-earths-land-surface-is-desert/*

- *www.zo.utexas.edu/courses/THOC/land.html*

- *www.ecofuture.org/pop/rpts/mccluney_maxpop.html*

Slate (Ben Blatt), "Manifest Destiny"

- *www.slate.com/articles/life/culturebox/2014/10/population_map_use_our_interactive_map_to_figure_out_how_many_flyover_states.html*

Trophic level interaction simulation

- *www.shodor.org/interactivate/activities/RabbitsAndWolves/*

U.S. Census Bureau Quick Facts

- *www.census.gov/quickfacts/fact/table/US/PST045221*

"Where We Live" map

- *www.globalrecruitingroundtable.com/wp-content/uploads/where-we-live-in-us.jpg*

"Wolves of Yellowstone: EARTH A New Wild"

- *http://oeta.pbslearningmedia.org/resource/a58e3ca2-52ab-45f5-87ac-26ee0d681146/wolves-of-yellowstone-earth-a-new-wild/*

Yellowstone National Park Trips "Wolf Introduction Changes Ecosystem in Yellowstone"

- *www.yellowstonepark.com/things-to-do/wildlife/wolf-reintroduction-changes-ecosystem/*

REFERENCES

Griffiths, A., & Grant, B. (1985). High school students' understanding of food webs: Identification of a learning hierarchy and related misconceptions. *Journal of Research in Science Teaching, 22*(5), 421–436.

Lesson Plan 2:
Impact of Population Density

In this lesson, students will examine the Earth's population density and the carrying capacity of the Earth and will explore the impact of the Earth's capacity limits on humans and their environment. Students will also explore some ways that scientists, technology experts, engineers, and mathematicians are addressing the issue of overpopulation and population density. Students will research the population density of their assigned endangered species to begin to understand the impact of population density on their assigned species.

ESSENTIAL QUESTIONS

- What is the population density of Earth?

- What percent of the Earth's surface is habitable?

- How much land is needed to support humans?

- What is the effect of population density on humans and the environment?

  - What are the psychological impacts on humans?

  - What are the physical impacts on humans?

  - What are the impacts on the environment?

- What is the population density of your assigned species?

- How does human population growth impact your assigned species and its habitat?

- What are some ways that scientists, technology experts, engineers, and mathematicians are addressing issues caused by population density?

ESTABLISHED GOALS AND OBJECTIVES

At the conclusion of this lesson, students will be able to do the following:

- Analyze and interpret data from static maps, interactive dynamic maps, data tables, and infographics to make and test conjectures about the population density of Earth and use this information to make conjectures about world population density

- Determine what percent of the Earth's surface is habitable and use that information to calculate how much land is needed to support humans

- Explore and determine psychological, physical, and environmental impacts of population density on humans and other species

- Understand the role that scientists, technology experts, engineers, and mathematicians play in addressing issues caused by high population density

- Explain how human population density impacts species

TIME REQUIRED

4 days (approximately 45 minutes each day; see Tables 3.6–3.7, p. 42)

MATERIALS

Required Materials for Lesson 2

- STEM Research Notebooks

- Computer, laptop, tablet, or other Internet-connected computing device (1 per student)

- Whiteboard or chart paper

- Presentation tools

- Calculators (1 per student)

- Graph paper (2 sheets per student)

- Digital storytelling app or website

- *Stronger than Steel: Spider Silk DNA and the Quest for Better Bulletproof Vests, Sutures, and Parachute Rope* (Scientists in the Field Series) by Bridget Heos

- One or more of the *Small Square* books by Donald Silver

- Poster board (1 per pair of students)

- Scissors (1 per pair of students)

- Markers (1 set per pair of students)

- Glue (1 per pair of students)

- Tape (1 per pair of students)

SAFETY NOTES

Students should use caution when handling scissors, as the sharp points and blades can cut or puncture skin.

CONTENT STANDARDS AND KEY VOCABULARY

Table 4.4 lists the content standards from the *NGSS*, *CCSS*, and the Framework for 21st Century Learning that this lesson addresses, and Table 4.5 (pp. 76–78) presents the key vocabulary. Vocabulary terms are provided for both teacher and student use. Teachers may choose to introduce some or all of the terms to students.

Table 4.4 Content Standards Addressed in STEM Road Map Module Lesson 2

NEXT GENERATION SCIENCE STANDARDS
PERFORMANCE OBJECTIVES
• MS-LS2–1. Ecosystems: Interactions, Energy, and Dynamics. Analyze and interpret data to provide evidence for the effects of resource availability on organisms and populations of organisms in an ecosystem.
• MS-LS2–2. Ecosystems: Interactions, Energy, and Dynamics. Construct an explanation that predicts patterns of interactions among organism across multiple ecosystems.
• MS-LS2–4. Ecosystems: Interactions, Energy, and Dynamics. Construct an argument supported by empirical evidence that changes to physical or biological components of an ecosystem affect populations.
SCIENCE AND ENGINEERING PRACTICES
Constructing Explanations and Designing Solutions
• Construct an explanation that includes qualitative or quantitative relationships between variables that predict phenomena.
Engaging in Argument from Evidence
• Construct an oral and written argument supported by empirical evidence and scientific reasoning to support or refute an explanation or a model for a phenomenon or a solution to a problem.
Analyzing and Interpreting Data
• Analyze and interpret data to provide evidence for phenomena.
Scientific Knowledge is Based on Empirical Evidence
• Science disciplines share common rules of obtaining and evaluating empirical evidence.
DISCIPLINARY CORE IDEAS
ESS3.C: Human Impacts on Earth Systems
• Typically as human populations and per-capita consumption of natural resources increase, so do the negative impacts on Earth unless the activities and technologies involved are engineered otherwise.
LS2.A: Interdependent Relationships in Ecosystems
• Organisms, and populations of organisms, are dependent on their environmental interactions both with other living things and with nonliving factors.
• In any ecosystem, organisms and populations with similar requirements for food, water, oxygen, or other resources may compete with each other for limited resources, access to which consequently constrains their growth and reproduction.
• Growth of organisms and population increases are limited by access to resources.

Table 4.4 (*continued*)

- Similarly, predatory interactions may reduce the number of organisms or eliminate whole populations of organisms. Mutually beneficial interactions, in contrast, may become so interdependent that each organism requires the other for survival. Although the species involved in these competitive, predatory, and mutually beneficial interactions vary across ecosystems, the patterns of interactions of organisms with their environments, both living and nonliving, are shared.

LS2.C: Ecosystem Dynamics, Functioning, and Resilience

- Ecosystems are dynamic in nature; their characteristics can vary over time. Disruptions to any physical or biological component of an ecosystem can lead to shifts in all its populations.

CROSSCUTTING CONCEPTS

Patterns

- Patterns can be used to identify cause and effect relationships.

Cause and Effect

- Cause and effect relationships may be used to predict phenomena in natural or designed systems.

Influence of Science, Engineering, and Technology on Society and the Natural World

- All human activity draws on natural resources and has both short and long-term consequences, positive as well as negative, for the health of people and the natural environment.

Stability and Change

- Small changes in one part of a system might cause large changes in another part.
- Science Addresses Questions About the Natural and Material World
- Scientific knowledge can describe the consequences of actions but does not necessarily prescribe the decisions that society takes.

COMMON CORE STATE STANDARDS FOR MATHEMATICS

MATHEMATICAL PRACTICES

- MP1. Make sense of problems and persevere in solving them.
- MP2. Reason abstractly and quantitatively.
- MP3. Construct viable arguments and critique the reasoning of others.
- MP4. Model with mathematics.
- MP5. Use appropriate tools strategically.
- MP6. Attend to precision.
- MP8. Look for and express regularity in repeated reasoning.

MATHEMATICAL CONTENT

- 7.SP.A.1. Understand that statistics can be used to gain information about a population by examining a sample of the population; generalizations about a population from a sample are valid only if the sample is representative of that population. Understand that random sampling tends to produce representative samples and support valid inferences.
- 7.SP.A.2. Use data from a random sample to draw inferences about a population with an unknown characteristic of interest. Generate multiple samples (or simulated samples) of the same size to gauge the variation in estimates or predictions. For example, estimate the mean word length in a book by randomly sampling words from the book; predict the winner of a school election based on randomly sampled survey data. Gauge how far off the estimate or prediction might be.

Table 4.4 (*continued*)

- 7.SP.B.3. Informally assess the degree of visual overlap of two numerical data distributions with similar variabilities, measuring the difference between the centers by expressing it as a multiple of a measure of variability.
- 7.SP.B.4. Use measures of center and measures of variability for numerical data from random samples to draw informal comparative inferences about two populations.

COMMON CORE STATE STANDARDS FOR ENGLISH LANGUAGE ARTS

READING STANDARDS

- RI.7.8. Trace and evaluate the argument and specific claims in a text, assessing whether the reasoning is sound and the evidence is relevant and sufficient to support the claims.
- RI.7.9. Analyze how two or more authors writing about the same topic shape their presentations of key information by emphasizing different evidence or advancing different interpretations of facts.

WRITING STANDARDS

- W.7.1. Write arguments to support claims with clear reasons and relevant evidence.
- W.7.1.a. Introduce claim(s), acknowledge alternate or opposing claims, and organize the reasons and evidence logically.
- W.7.1.b. Support claim(s) with logical reasoning and relevant evidence, using accurate, credible sources and demonstrating an understanding of the topic or text.
- W.7.1.c. Use words, phrases, and clauses to create cohesion and clarify the relationships among claim(s), reasons, and evidence.
- W.7.1.e. Provide a concluding statement or section that follows from and supports the argument presented.
- W.7.2. Write informative/explanatory texts to examine a topic and convey ideas, concepts, and information through the selection, organization, and analysis of relevant content.
- W.7.2.a. Introduce a topic clearly, previewing what is to follow; organize ideas, concepts, and information, using strategies such as definition, classification, comparison/contrast, and cause/effect; include formatting (e.g., headings), graphics (e.g., charts, tables), and multimedia when useful to aiding comprehension.
- W.7.2.b. Develop the topic with relevant facts, definitions, concrete details, quotations, or other information and examples.
- W.7.2.d. Use precise language and domain-specific vocabulary to inform about or explain the topic.
- W.7.3.c. Use a variety of transition words, phrases, and clauses to convey sequence and signal shifts from one time frame or setting to another.
- W.7.6. Use technology, including the Internet, to produce and publish writing and link to and cite sources as well as to interact and collaborate with others, including linking to and citing sources.
- W.7.7. Conduct short research projects to answer a question, drawing on several sources and generating additional related, focused questions for further research and investigation.
- W.7.8. Gather relevant information from multiple print and digital sources, using search terms effectively; assess the credibility and accuracy of each source; and quote or paraphrase the data and conclusions of others while avoiding plagiarism and following a standard format for citation.
- W.7.9. Draw evidence from literary or informational texts to support analysis, reflection, and research.

Table 4.4 (*continued*)

SPEAKING AND LISTENING STANDARDS • SL.7.1. Engage effectively in a range of collaborative discussions (one-on-one, in groups, and teacher-led) with diverse partners on grade 7 topics, texts, and issues, building on others' ideas and expressing their own clearly. • SL.7.1.a. Come to discussions prepared, having read or researched material under study; explicitly draw on that preparation by referring to evidence on the topic, text, or issue to probe and reflect on ideas under discussion. • SL.7.1.b. Follow rules for collegial discussions, track progress toward specific goals and deadlines, and define individual roles as needed. • SL.7.1.c. Pose questions that elicit elaboration and respond to others' questions and comments with relevant observations and ideas that bring the discussion back on topic as needed. • SL.7.1.d. Acknowledge new information expressed by others and, when warranted, modify their own views. • SL.7.3. Delineate a speaker's argument and specific claims, evaluating the soundness of the reasoning and the relevance and sufficiency of the evidence. • SL.7.4. Present claims and findings, emphasizing salient points in a focused, coherent manner with pertinent descriptions, facts, details, and examples; use appropriate eye contact, adequate volume, and clear pronunciation. • SL.7.5. Include multimedia components and visual displays in presentations to clarify claims and findings and emphasize salient points. *FRAMEWORK FOR 21ST CENTURY LEARNING* • Global Awareness • Environmental Literacy • Civic Literacy • Creativity and Innovation • Critical Thinking and Problem Solving • Communication and Collaboration • Information Literacy • Media Literacy • ICT Literacy

Table 4.5 Key Vocabulary in Lesson 2

Key Vocabulary for Students	Definition
aquaponics	a system for producing food that combines raising aquatic animals (e.g., fish) in tanks with cultivating plants in water; the animals produce waste that then supplies nutrients to the plants grown hydroponically
carrying capacity	the number of living things that a region can support without environmental degradation

Table 4.5 (*continued*)

Key Vocabulary for Students	Definition
cisgenic	a GMO that has only been modified with genes from its own species
competition	interaction between groups or individuals in which each strives for access to limited resources such as food, water, or living space
desertification	when an area of land becomes a desert
exponential population growth	unrestricted population growth occurs in the absence of any limiting factors
food desert	a geographic area (often urban) in which it is difficult to buy affordable or good-quality fresh food
food security	according to the World Food Summit (1996), food security exists "when all people at all times have access to sufficient, safe, nutritious food to maintain a healthy and active life" and is built on three pillars: food availability, food access, and food use (*www.worldbank.org/en/topic/agriculture/brief/food-security-update/what-is-food-security*)
food swamp	a geographic area where high-energy, processed foods are more abundant and accessible than healthy food options
genetically modified organism (GMO)	an organism whose genetic make-up has been manipulated through genetic engineering to create a new or desirable characteristics; often used in biological research, pharmaceuticals, and agriculture
limiting factors	any basic requirement that restricts the growth of a population (e.g., available food, shelter, increased density, disease, competition); limiting factors can be biotic or abiotic
logistic population growth	when the growth rate of the population slows as the number of individuals increases, usually as a result of resource limitations
over-irrigation	supplying too much water to crops; can result in crop diseases and weed problems
predation	act of one organism feeding on another
salinization	build-up of salt in the soil
soil degradation	change in soil caused by improper use or overuse, usually for agricultural or industrial purposes or for urban development (*https://foodinsight.org/preserving-the-worlds-land-from-soil-degradation/*)
sustainable intensification	increasing food production from farmland while minimizing the environmental impacts of farming
transgenic	a GMO that has been modified with genes from another species

Table 4.5 (*continued*)

Key Vocabulary for Students	Definition
vertical farming	cultivating crops in vertical stacks rather than over large stretches of field; often associated with urban agriculture and often using artificial light and climate control
water pollution	addition of harmful chemicals to water
water security	reliable access to adequate quantities and quality of water for the population of a species

TEACHER BACKGROUND INFORMATION

This lesson provides an opportunity for students to explore population density around the world and to examine factors caused by population density. The following information will be useful for background for this lesson.

Population growth generally, regardless of density, has implications for human behavior in the long term that scientists, engineers, and sociologists continue to grapple with. For example, the National Geographic provides information about the implications of feeding the world with a growing population at *www.nationalgeographic.com/foodfeatures/feeding-9-billion/*. This information indicates that crop production must double by 2050 in order to feed the world's human population, suggesting the need for technological innovations in food production and distribution.

In addition to issues such as food production associated with population growth generally, growing population density has numerous implications for both human and non-human life. According to the Rewilding Institute (2015) (*https://rewilding.org/our-programs/population-growth/*), there are five types of consequences of population growth:

- Land abuse and loss of productivity

- Depletion of natural resources and conflict over obtaining new sources

- Inability to grow enough food, which leads to hunger and famine

- Social, economic, and security crises and threats

- Harm to nature

Although research suggests that, in the US, population density is positively correlated with household incomes in urban areas, this relationship does not hold with situations of overcrowding or for all demographic groups of people. Importantly, research indicates that "institutional and historical limitations on some racial groups, particularly people of color, stunt the growth in income that may occur from the co-location of people and homes" (Hummel, 2020, p. 43). This highlights the numerous social justice issues that may impact people with low socioeconomic status living in areas of high population density, including the prevalence of food deserts, or areas where people have limited access to healthy foods (Mead, 2008), less access to healthcare (Cyr et al., 2019), and the persistence of generational poverty (Butler & Grabinsky, 2020). These impacts are particularly troubling since global population growth is concentrated in urban areas with relatively high population densities, with the number of people living in urban areas projected to grow from about 4.4 billion in 2020 to 6.7 billion in 2050 (United Nations, 2020). It is important to recognize and be alert to these issues and understand the complexity of how the demographics of students' settings can impact their lives and their understandings of global population issues. Students will explore the implications of high human population densities in this lesson. You should be prepared to discuss with students how these issues relate to your particular context and how students in other settings might experience these issues.

Research indicates that high population density can have other negative effects on humans, including the following:

- High population density has psychological and physical effects on humans. "High urban density fosters a sense of competition, reserve, loneliness, and irritation" (Fischer, 1972; Milgram, 1970; Wirth, 1938).

- As population density increases, "space for activities and easy movement decreases; privacy and quiet decrease; property control and predictability of local events decrease" (Taylor & Verbrugge, 1980, p. 137).

- Noise pollution can also be a negative effect of population density (Page, 1977).

- Noise can impact the nervous system, and can cause gastrointestinal problems and anxiety (Veitrich & Arkkatelin, 1995). Engineers have created structures to dampen the impacts of noise on humans and other animals. For example, engineers and scientists have created soundproof glass and double doors in homes and buildings, installed sound buffers on highways, and created noise-reduction building materials.

- Densely populated areas tend to have a higher crime rate than sparsely populated communities. Animals other than humans often experience what Calhoun (1962) called behavioral sink. This is a situation where reproductive habits and normal behavior change, and animals become more aggressive as they compete for resources.

- Natural disasters can cause more deaths and damage in densely populated areas. Additionally, disease and other health-related issues spread more rapidly in densely populated areas.

There can also be positive effects of living in a densely populated area. Researchers have shown that areas with high population density may have access to more social resources. In addition, careful planning of large urban areas can significantly reduce the psychological and physical effects of population density. Measures that planners can take include the following:

- Urban planners can limit some loss of biodiversity by increasing the amount of green spaces in large cities (for more information see *https://climate-adapt.eea.europa.eu/en/metadata/adaptation-options/green-spaces-and-corridors-in-urban-areas/#source*)

- Scientists, engineers, and mathematicians can use technology to predict future population density.

- Genetically modified organisms (GMOs) can be a way to increase food production; information about GMOs including a timeline of GMO is available at *www.greenamerica.org/blog/gmo-timeline-history-genetically-modified-foods*.

In science class, students will consider the effect of sea lice on salmon populations. You should familiarize yourself with the causes and implications of this issue. There are a number of articles and resources available online about this topic that can be accessed using a Google search. Examples include the following:

- Halifax Examiner, "Sea Lice are Decimating Atlantic Salmon, and Climate Change is Making it Worse" at www.halifaxexaminer.ca/environment/sea-lice-are-decimating-atlantic-salmon-and-climate-change-is-making-the-situation-worse/

- Natural History Museum, "The Problem of Sea Lice in Salmon Farms" at *www.nhm.ac.uk/discover/the-problem-of-sea-lice-in-salmon-farms.html*

- Alaska Department of Fish and Game, "What Are Sea Lice?" at www.adfg.alaska.gov/index.cfm?adfg=wildlifenews.view_article&articles_id=388

- Seafood Source, "The Sticky Problem of Sea Lice – And What's Being Done to Stop Them" at www.seafoodsource.com/news/aquaculture/the-sticky-problem-of-sea-lice-and-what-s-being-done-to-stop-them

COMMON MISCONCEPTIONS

Students will have various types of prior knowledge about the concepts introduced in this lesson. Table 4.6 outlines common misconceptions students may have concerning these concepts. Because of the breadth of students' experiences, it is not possible to anticipate every misconception that students may bring as they approach this lesson. Incorrect or inaccurate prior understanding of concepts can influence student learning in the future, however, so it is important to be alert to misconceptions such as those presented in the table.

Table 4.6 Common Misconceptions About the Concepts in Lesson 2

Topic	Student Misconception	Explanation
Population growth	A small population growth rate means that the population is barely growing.	Because the world population is very large, even a small percentage in growth represents a large number of individuals. With a world population of about 8 billion people, a growth rate of less than 1% means that the population of the world grows by tens of millions of people each year. For example, with a growth rate of about.8%, the population grows by 67 million each year and, at this rate, the world's population would double in 83 years.
	The growth in the world's population is not a matter for concern because of technological innovations that allow for increased food production.	Although new technologies have allowed for increased food production and better means of distribution, these practices have environmental implications including increasing energy demands, air and water pollution, the production of greenhouse gases, plastic waste, and decreasing crop diversity.

PREPARATION FOR LESSON 2

Review the Teacher Background Information provided (pp. 78–80), assemble the materials for the lesson, and preview the video and websites recommended in the Learning Plan Components section that follows.

Students will investigate world population growth. One tool the class will use is the Our World in Data "World Population Growth" website at *http://ourworldindata.org/data/population-growth-vital-statistics/world-population-growth/*. You should review this site and become familiar with the graphs.

The class will discuss the impact of the bubonic plague on population density. Be prepared to discuss the impact of the plague on European nations' populations in the short term (large impacts) and in the long term (less impact). Review resources such as the following:

- Britannica, "Effects and Significance" at *www.britannica.com/event/Black-Death/Effects-and-significance*

- Khan Academy, "Bubonic Plague" at *www.khanacademy.org/humanities/world-history/medieval-times/disease-and-demography/a/disease-and-demograpy*

- VOX EU, "Pandemics, Places, and Populations: Evidence from the Black Death" at *https://voxeu.org/article/how-black-death-changed-europes-cities*

Adrienne Redmond-Sanogo et al.

You should also become familiar with ways to create digital stories, including apps or websites (for example, see Tech Learning's "Best Sites and Apps for Digital Storytelling" at *www.techlearning.com/tl-advisor-blog/30-sites-and-apps-for-digital-storytelling* and eLearning Industry's "18 Free Digital Storytelling Tools for Teachers and Students" at *http://elearningindustry.com/free-digital-storytelling-tools-for-teachers-and-students*).

As noted in the Teacher Background section of this lesson, the issues with global population density that students will investigate in this lesson have numerous implications for social justice and equity. You may wish to access current news articles or other resources to use in class discussions of these issues. Social studies teachers may find opportunities to connect these issues with curricular content regarding the historical roots of and trends in social inequity, demographic issues, and other content.

LEARNING PLAN COMPONENTS
Introductory Activity/Engagement

Connection to the Challenge: Begin each day of this lesson by directing students' attention to the module challenge. Remind students that, working in teams, they will determine an appropriate mathematical model to measure the population of their team's assigned species. Hold a brief class discussion each day of how students' learning in the previous days' lessons contributed to their ability to complete the challenge. You may wish to create a class list of key ideas on chart paper.

Science Class: Students will consider the effects of sea lice on salmon populations. Tell students scientific studies have showed that salmon populations are being impacted by sea lice.

Show a video about the effect of sea lice on salmon populations such as the following (be sure to provide students with the questions listed below to think about prior to watching): *www.youtube.com/watch?v=FvTZ3x61kFk*. After the video, use a think, pair, share strategy and have students answer the following questions:

- What is happening to the salmon population?

- What role do salmon open-net farms play in this problem?

- What does this have to do with population density?

- If we were to graph the salmon population in an open-net farm over time, what would this graph look like? (Have students work in pairs to create the graph and describe what is happening.)

- What about the sea lice population? What would that graph look like?

Sketch the following graph on a whiteboard or on chart paper. Ask students what is happening in the first part of the graph. Make sure students note that growth starts off at a slow pace, then increases, then levels off, and finally starts to decline. Introduce the concepts of carrying capacity and limiting factors.

Figure 4.2 Graph of Salmon Population Changes Over Time

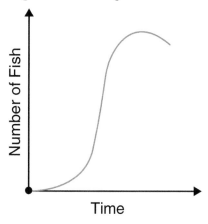

Hold a class discussion about the graph, asking the following questions:

- What do you think happened in each phase? Why does this number of fish level off?

- Why does the number of fish start decreasing?

- Where do you think the carrying capacity of this ecosystem was reached?

- What were the limiting factors in this ecosystem?

- If this were happening to the salmon, what would be happening to the population of the sea lice in this ecosystem?

- What impact will the extinction of salmon have on the ecosystem? (Remind students of the reintroduction of wolves in Yellowstone.)

- What are some things that scientists, technology experts, engineers, and mathematicians can do to solve this problem? (Take suggestions from students.)

Next, introduce the terms biotic and abiotic. Hold a class discussion about the difference between biotic (e.g., predation, availability of plants for food) and abiotic factors (e.g., temperature, moisture) that affect species. Discuss what biotic and abiotic factors are at work in the situation with salmon.

Next, show students a video about fish farming using cages or geodesic domes such as "Mobile Fish Farms Could Soon Navigate the Oceans" at *www.youtube.com/watch?v=DCz1KNBI60I* and/or "Deep Sea Fish Farming with Geodesic Domes" at *www.youtube.com/watch?v=NSZV_Ikrg0s&t=471s*.

Discuss the video(s), asking students the following:

- Would the approach you saw in the video be a solution for the salmon population? Why? Why not?

- What are some other solutions?

STEM Research Notebook Entry

Have students answer the following prompt in their STEM Research Notebook:

- What role do you think population density is playing in the death of salmon?

- What biotic factors are impacting the salmon population?

- What abiotic factors are impacting the salmon population?

- What role do you think humans are playing in the death of salmon?

- What creative solution would you develop to prevent the extinction of salmon?

Revisit students' previous STEM Research Notebook entries. Ask students the following questions:

- What did we learn about the carrying capacity of the salmon net farm ecosystems?

- What were the limiting factors for the salmon?

- Which were abiotic and which were biotic?

- What are some limiting factors for your team's assigned species?

- What are limiting factors for the carrying capacity of Earth?

What is the carrying capacity of Earth? How many people do you think the Earth can support? Can that figure change with technological innovations?

Access a world population counter such as the Worldometer "Current World Population" counter at *www.worldometers.info/world-population/*. Give students time to study the numbers ticking on the screen. Ask students the following questions:

- Do you notice any trends in the numbers presented here? (Make sure that students note that humans are being born at a faster rate than people are dying, resulting in population growth.)

- Why do you think the population is growing so fast now?

- Are there any limiting factors to human population growth? What are some limiting factors that the human population can/will experience?

- Were the limiting factors for early humans different? How so?

Ask students if they have heard of the "Black Death" or bubonic plague. Tell students that this was a pandemic that impacted Europe and Asia in the mid-1300s, killing about 25 million people, including as much as 40% of Europe's population. Ask students to consider what impact that event had on population density and hold a class discussion asking students to share their ideas about what areas (e.g., urban or rural) might have been affected the most, and whether those impacts were still evident after 20 years went by and after 100 years went by. Hold a class discussion about the impact of technology and medicine on the human population and population density.

Next, have students work in teams to explore these questions.

- How much land is required to sustain one human life?

- What type of resources and how much of those resources are needed to sustain the life of your assigned species?

Have students come back together as a class and share their findings.

STEM Research Notebook Entry

Have students respond to the following questions in their STEM Research Notebooks:

- What are abiotic and biotic limiting factors for your species?

- Figuring out how to feed the world's population is one of our greatest challenges as a species; what suggestions do you have for addressing the challenge?

Are GMOs the Answer?

Next, introduce genetically modified organisms (GMOs) to students by telling them that some scientists believe that GMOs are the best way to feed the growing human population. Share a video about GMOs with students, such as "What Is a Genetically Modified Food—Instant Egghead #45" at *www.youtube.com/watch?v=JMPE5wlB3Zk*.

Next, share the book *Stronger than Steel: Spider Silk DNA and the Quest for Better Bulletproof Vests, Sutures, and Parachute Rope* (Scientists in the Field Series) by Bridget Heos with students. Hold a class discussion about GMOs, asking students the following:

- What are some interesting transgenic organisms that you think would be helpful for us? Why?

- Is it ethical or safe to create GMOs?

Tell students that there is a debate whether we should create GMOs and that some countries have already banned GMO use. Have students work in pairs to conduct Internet research about what GMOs are and the arguments for and against using them as a tool to solve the world food crisis. Tell students that they will each choose a side of the debate and present their arguments using digital storytelling. You may wish to display these digital arguments on your class webpage and have students share them with their parents, members of the community, and local agencies.

Have students connect GMOs to their assigned species by creating a STEM Research Notebook entry in which they consider genetic modifications to their assigned species.

STEM Research Notebook Entry

Have students respond to the following in their STEM Research Notebooks: What are some helpful and harmful genetic modifications that could be made to your assigned species? Create a table listing the pros and cons of genetically modifying your organism.

Mathematics Class: Show students a video about the growth of the human population such as "World Population" at https://vimeo.com/130468614. Hold a class discussion about what the growth in population means for population density.

Have students work in teams to investigate human population density. Instruct teams to brainstorm what information they would need to calculate the world's human

population density. Have teams share with the class their ideas about how they would calculate population density, creating a class list of ideas and needed information. Students should mention that they need to know the area of land on Earth and the world's population. If they do not suggest it, ask prompting questions such as:

- What did you need to know to calculate the population density of the states you explored?

- How many people live on Earth?

- How much of Earth is habitable?

- How much of the Earth's surface is covered by oceans?

- How much of the Earth's surface is covered by desert and mountains?

- What about lakes and other fresh bodies of water?

Have student pairs conduct research on the above topics and work to calculate the human population density of the Earth. Tell students that while doing research they should be sure to determine what percentage of the Earth's surface is covered by water (oceans, mountains, fresh bodies of water such as lakes and streams) and how much is desert. Have students record the information they gathered and their calculations in their STEM Research Notebooks.

STEM Research Notebook Entry

Have students record the findings from their research (the population of Earth, the amount of habitable land, and other information) and their calculations for human population density in their STEM Research Notebooks.

After student pairs have explored these questions for about 20–30 minutes, completed their calculations, and recorded the information in their STEM Research Notebooks, bring them back together for a class discussion of their findings. In your whole-class discussion, have student pairs share their findings. Ask students to respond to the following questions after the discussion:

- Did everyone come up with the same solutions? Why? Why not?

- How do you think human population density has changed over time?

Next, Visit the Our World in Data "World Population Growth" website at http://ourworldindata.org/data/population-growth-vital-statistics/world-population-growth/. Show the "How has world population growth changed over time?" graph. Ask students the following questions:

- What do you notice about the graph?

- What do you think the population density was in the year 100?

- Why do think the population is rising so fast now?

- What do you think will happen in the future?

Show students the Our World in Data graph, "Population and Projected Growth (Total Population and Under 5), World, 1950 to 2100" at *https://ourworldindata.org/grapher/ world-population-and-projected-growth-to-2100-total-population-and-under-age-5*.

Ask students what they notice about the graph. Next, show students the "Population Density" graph at *https://ourworldindata.org/grapher/population-density?tab=chart&c ountry=CIV~COD~DJI~DOM~DNK~DMA~SXM*. Work together as a class to answer the following questions using the graphs:

- What is the estimated human population in 2100?

- What is the estimated population density of humans in 2100?

- Why do humans need to know about the human population density?

- What implications will this population and population density have on humans and their environment?

Next, have students consider what factors could impact the population density of their species and create a STEM Research Notebook entry to connect their understanding of human population density to their assigned species.

STEM Research Notebook Entry

Have students respond to the following questions in their STEM Research Notebooks: What factors could impact the population density of your species? What is the impact of population density on your assigned species?

Next, access a current infographic about world population such as the Population Reference Bureau's "World Population Data Sheet" (the most current infographics can be accessed at *www.prb.org/collections/data-sheets/*). Review the infographic as a class, asking the following questions:

- How is this different than the population representations we discussed previously?

- What does this data have to do with population density?

Have student pairs explore the Population Reference Bureau "World Population Data" interactive infographic accessed from *www.prb.org/collections/data-sheets/*. Have students record answers to the following questions in their STEM Research Notebooks:

- How does this interactive infographic display information?

- What is the population of North America predicted to be (record the year and the prediction)?

- How does that compare to what the population is now?

- What will be the effect of this on population density?

Next, assign each pair of students three countries to research; assign countries so that a variety of continents are represented. Give students the following directions:

- Calculate the percentage of the world's population that each country represents in the most recent year for which there is data and the percent it will represent in 2050 (or a year about 30 years in the future). Was there a change? Why do you think there was a change, or no change?

- What is the population density of each country in the most recent year for which there is data and what will it be in 2050? Was there a change? Why do you think there was a change, or no change?

Bring students back together and have them share their findings in a class table. Choose students to share why they believe their countries changed or didn't change in population density.

STEM Research Notebook Entry

Have students respond to the following prompts in their STEM Research Notebook. Do we have enough resources to sustain the world's population in 2050? Discuss your answer in detail. Does your assigned species have enough resources to sustain its population? Why? Why not?

ELA Connection: These ELA connections will span the entire lesson. Use one or more of the *Small Square* books by Donald Silver, all of which show the wildlife that exists in a square meter of various habitats, to support learning to "write small." You may wish to refer to *Craft Lessons: Teaching Writing K–8* by Ralph Fletcher and Jo Ann Portalupi for various lessons on using detail, finding focus, etc.

Call attention to the various ways nonfiction writers use graphics to communicate information. Allow students to explore various texts to identify forms of graphics and examine their purposes. Share and discuss what information might be gleaned from each and what readers need to know and notice (labels, relational features such as axes, coding systems, units, and directionality).

Challenge small groups of students to translate a graphic to text, trying to express in words what the graphic communicates visually. Discuss the results together, asking: Why might an author choose a graphic rather than a text? And vice versa? Display a variety of infographics, engaging students in discussions about what information might be gleaned from each. Have students consider labels, relational features, coding systems, and directionality. Consider using the findings from this exploration to compose together a guide to reading infographics.

To help students understand why an author might choose a graphic rather than a strictly textual explanation, challenge them to translate a graphic to text, seeking to express in words all the information contained in the graphic. Students may benefit from doing this work in pairs or small groups. Discuss the challenge results together.

Social Studies Connection:

Ask students to respond to the following questions:

- What is the population density of our classroom?

- Do you feel we have enough room to move around?

- Are there enough resources for everyone?

- What if our class population doubled – what would be our population density?

- Do you feel we would have enough room to move around then?

- Would there be enough resources for everyone? Why? Why not?

- What additional resources would we need?

- What if the class population doubled again the next day?

Show students the following visual simulation of the class size doubling over three days:

Figure 4.3 Visual Simulation of Class Size Doubliing Over Three Days

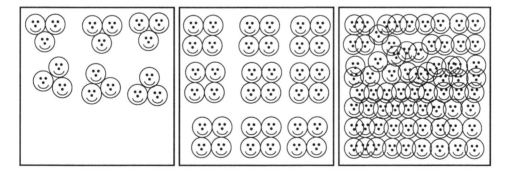

- What would be the physical and psychological impacts of the class size doubling for two straight days? How would you feel if you were in the classroom on the far right?

Tell students that they will work in pairs to explore the positive and negative impacts of high population density on humans. Each pair should create a list of these factors and share this list with the class. Give students an opportunity to conduct Internet research and create a list of positive and negative impacts. Negative impacts include

competition, loneliness, irritation, anxiety, privacy issues, noise pollution, higher crime rate, less biodiversity, aggression increases, access to food, access to water, food security, and food deserts and swamps. Positive impacts include more social and educational resources and better urban planning.

Bring students back together and create a master list of both positive and negative impacts of high population density. Ask students:

- Which of these negative impacts concern you the most? Why? Why not? (If students don't mention food and water security, you should ask a question to bring it up.)

- What are scientists, technology experts, engineers, and mathematicians doing to address these issues?

Population Density Issue Posters

List the following issues on a whiteboard or chart paper: food security, desertification, water security, noise pollution, food waste, and waste disposal. Divide the students up into pairs and give them one of these issues to explore using the Internet. Tell students that they will need to become experts on their issue. They will need to determine the following and record their findings in their STEM Research Notebooks:

- Why this is an issue.

- What scientists, engineers, technology experts, and mathematicians are doing to address the issue.

- What specific fields in science, technology, engineering, and mathematics are addressing the issue.

- How they would solve the issue themselves, and why.

ave each pair partner with another student pair who had the same issue and share their information, answering the following questions: What is similar? What is different?

Have each pair of students prepare a poster to share their findings with the class. Place the group posters around the room and have students do a gallery walk around the room. As they walk around, have them answer the following questions in their STEM Research Notebooks for each issue:

- What was interesting?

- What was surprising?

- What are you still curious about?

- What are some ways that you would address the issue?

Explanation

Science Class and Social Studies Connections: Hold a whole-class discussion about the population density issue posters. Use student work to address specific gaps in knowledge and misconceptions present in their findings.

Next, present students with the following challenge:

You are an urban planner. You and your team have been hired by the President to create a new megacity to address issues of overpopulation, sustainability, waste disposal, noise pollution, water safety, and food safety. Your megacity must be people friendly and self-sustaining. There must be an adequate amount of green spaces (parks) and your plan must use vertical gardening, aquaponics, edible landscaping, zero-scaping, and other eco-friendly means of feeding the population. The city can only use clean sources of energy. You will create a poster of your ideas and present it to a panel. You will need to include information about the impact of population density on humans and the environment in your presentation.

STEM Research Notebook Entry

Have students respond to the following question in their STEM Research Notebooks: If you were going to create a specialized "city" for your species, how would you change their habitat?

Mathematics Class: Access the "Per Square Mile" infographic by Tim De Chant at *http://persquaremile.com/2011/01/18/if-the-worlds-population-lived-in-one-city/*. Have students examine the infographic and ask them what this we can learn from it. Have students explore the infographic and make conjectures, answering the following questions:

- What would this look like five years from now?

- How did the author create this infographic? How did he calculate the amount of space?

- What is missing from this infographic?

Access the infographics for various countries at Per Square Mile, "If the World's Population Lived Like…" page at *http://persquaremile.com/2012/08/08/if-the-worlds-population-lived-like/*. Show the students the information about how much land would be required if each nation lived like one of the nations listed. Ask students how much land would be necessary if the world's population lived like the USA (as of 2022, it would take 4.1 Earths to sustain the population). Have students look at a variety of other nations such as France, China, and the United Arab Emirates. Ask students to answer the following question in their STEM Research Notebooks: What can we learn about the impact of population density on humans and the environment from this infographic?

Adrienne Redmond-Sanogo et al.

ELA Connection: N.A.
Social Studies Connection: N.A.

Elaboration/Application of Knowledge

Science Class: Optional extensions include the following: Connect to students' learning about GMOs by focusing on the genetic material of plants. Tell students that before scientists can alter the DNA of plants to create new seeds to create plants with different characteristics, they must first understand the genetic code of the plant. Use a resource such as the Utah Farm Bureau's "Strawberry DNA Activity" at *www.utahfarmbureau. org/Article/Strawberry-DNA-Activity* to have students learn about DNA and extract DNA from strawberries.

Mathematics Class: Introduce exponential growth using a resource such as Population Education's "Population Riddles" at *https://populationeducation.org/resource/population-riddles/*. Have students identify examples of exponential growth and exponential decay.

ELA Connection: Conduct a writing workshop. Environmental and social issues can tap into young people's natural sense of justice and need for action and, thus, lend themselves to a variety of authentic reading connections and writing responses. Work with students to determine ways to use their literacy skills to respond to what they are learning. A menu of choices might include using persuasive writing skills to communicate to policy makers about a need for change in urban planning, writing, and submitting a proposal for a project they want to complete (like creating a school garden), or writing books sharing what they know with others. Make sure you articulate with learners the various literacy skills involved and create (ideally together) a plan for teaching/learning those skills and a rubric to assess them.

Evaluation/Assessment

Students may be assessed on the following performance tasks and other measures listed.

Performance Tasks

- Are GMOs the Answer? Digital storytelling (rubric)

- Population Density Issue posters (rubric)

Other Measures

- STEM Research Notebook entries

- Participation in class discussions

INTERNET RESOURCES

Bubonic plague, population effects

- *www.britannica.com/event/Black-Death/Effects-and-significance*
- *www.khanacademy.org/humanities/world-history/medieval-times/disease-and-demography/a/disease-and-demograpy*
- *https://voxeu.org/article/how-black-death-changed-europes-cities*

Consequences of population growth

- *https://rewilding.org/our-programs/population-growth/ www.nationalgeographic.com/foodfeatures/feeding-9-billion/*
- *http://ec.europa.eu/environment/integration/research/newsalert/pdf/51na4_en.pdf*

Digital storytelling resources

- *www.techlearning.com/tl-advisor-blog/30-sites-and-apps-for-digital-storytelling*
- *http://elearningindustry.com/free-digital-storytelling-tools-for-teachers-and-student*

Fish farming innovation videos

- *www.youtube.com/watch?v=DCz1KNBI60I*
- *www.youtube.com/watch?v=NSZV_Ikrg0s&t=471s*

GMOs

- *www.greenamerica.org/blog/gmo-timeline-history-genetically-modified-foods*
- *www.youtube.com/watch?v=JMPE5wlB3Zk*

Our World in Data graphs

- *http://ourworldindata.org/data/population-growth-vital-statistics/world-population-growth/*
- *https://ourworldindata.org/grapher/world-population-and-projected-growth-to-2100-total-population-and-under-age-5*
- *https://ourworldindata.org/grapher/population-density?tab=chart&country=CIV~COD~DJI~DOM~DNK~DMA~SXM*

"Per Square Mile" (Tim De Chant) resources

- *http://persquaremile.com/2011/01/18/if-the-worlds-population-lived-in-one-city/*
- *http://persquaremile.com/2012/08/08/if-the-worlds-population-lived-like/*

Population Education's classroom resources

- *https://populationeducation.org/teacher-resources/?_sft_resource_type=tool*

Population Education's "Population Riddles"

- *https://populationeducation.org/resource/population-riddles/*

Population Reference Bureau resources

- *www.prb.org/collections/data-sheets/*

Salmon and sea lice

- *www.halifaxexaminer.ca/environment/sea-lice-are-decimating-atlantic-salmon-and-climate-change-is-making-the-situation-worse/*

- *www.nhm.ac.uk/discover/the-problem-of-sea-lice-in-salmon-farms.html*

- *www.adfg.alaska.gov/index.cfm?adfg=wildlifenews.view_article&articles_id=388*

- *www.seafoodsource.com/news/aquaculture/the-sticky-problem-of-sea-lice-and-what-s-being-done-to-stop-them*

- *www.youtube.com/watch?v=FvTZ3x61kFk*

Utah Farm Bureau's "Strawberry DNA Activity"

- *www.utahfarmbureau.org/Article/Strawberry-DNA-Activity*

Worldometer "Current World Population" counter

- *www.worldometers.info/world-population/*

"World Population" video

- *https://vimeo.com/130468614*

REFERENCES

Butler, S. M., & Grabinsky, J. (2020). *Tackling the legacy of persistent urban inequality and concentrated poverty*. Brookings Institution. www.brookings.edu/blog/up-front/2020/11/16/tackling-the-legacy-of-persistent-urban-inequality-and-concentrated-poverty/

Calhoun, J. B. (1962). Population density and social pathology. *Scientific American*, 206(3), 139–148.

Cyr, M. E., Etchin, A. G., Guthrie, B. J., & Benneyan, J. C. (2019). Access to specialty healthcare in urban versus rural US populations: A systematic literature review. *BMC Health Services Research*, 19(1), 1–17.

Fischer, C. S. (1972). Urbanism as a way of life: A review and an agenda. *Sociology Methods and Research*, 1, 187–242.

Hummel, D. (2020). The effects of population and housing density in urban areas on income in the United States. *Local Economy*, *35*(1), 27–47.

Mead, M. N. (2008). Urban issues: The sprawl of food deserts. *Environmental Health Perspectives*, *116*(8).

Milgram, S. (1970). The experience of living in cities, *Science*, *167*, 1461–1468.

Page, R. A. (1977). Effects of noise on people. *Journal of the Acoustical Society of America*, *56*, 729–764.

Taylor, R. B., & Verbrugge, L. M. (1980). Consequences of population density and size. *Urban Affairs Quarterly*, *16*, 135–160.

United Nations (2020, February 21). Urbanization: Expanding opportunities, but deeper divides. United Nations Department of Economic and Social Affairs. www.un.org/development/desa/en/news/social/urbanization-expanding-opportunities-but-deeper-divides.html

Veitrich, R., & Arkkatelin, D. (1995). *Environmental psychology perspective*. Prentice Hall.

Wirth, L. (1938). Urbanism as a way of life. *American Journal of Sociology*, *44*, 1–24.

Adrienne Redmond-Sanogo et al.

Lesson Plan 3:
Exploring Sampling and Making
Generalizations and Inferences

In this lesson, students will investigate population sampling, determine if a sample is representative of the population, and learn about generalizing from a sample and making inferences. Students will continue to explore the population density of their assigned species and begin to think about how they will determine the population density of their species.

ESSENTIAL QUESTIONS

- What is a sample?

- What are sampling techniques?

- What sampling techniques are appropriate to use?

- How do we determine if a sample is representative?

- How do we make generalizations from a sample to the population?

- What is an inference and how can we make inferences from a set of data?

ESTABLISHED GOALS AND OBJECTIVES

At the conclusion of this lesson, students will be able to do the following:

- Define the term "sample" and understand the difference between population and sample

- Explain the reason for using sampling techniques and offer one or two examples

- Identify how to choose an appropriate sampling technique based on a research question

- Determine if a sample is representative of the population under investigation

- Make generalizations from a sample and apply those to the population

- Determine when it is and isn't appropriate to make inferences about a set of data

TIME REQUIRED

10 days (approximately 45 minutes each day; see Tables 3.7–3.9, pp. 42–43)

MATERIALS

Required Materials for Lesson 3

- STEM Research Notebooks
- Laptops (or other tablet or computer), presentation tools, and software
- Markers (1 set per student)
- Scissors (1 per student)
- Posterboard (1 per student)
- Tape (1 per student)
- Red and green colored counters (25 red and 15 green) (1 set per group of 4 students)
- Lunch-size paper bags (1 per group of 4 students)

SAFETY NOTES

Students should use caution when handling scissors, as the sharp points and blades can cut or puncture skin.

CONTENT STANDARDS AND KEY VOCABULARY

Table 4.7 lists the content standards from the *Next Generation Science Standards* (*NGSS*), *Common Core State Standards* (*CCSS*), and the Framework for 21st Century Learning that this lesson addresses, and Table 4.8 (p. 101) presents the key vocabulary. Vocabulary terms are provided for both teacher and student use. Teachers may choose to introduce some or all of the terms to students.

Table 4.7 Content Standards Addressed in STEM Road Map Module Lesson 3

NEXT GENERATION SCIENCE STANDARDS

PERFORMANCE OBJECTIVES
- MS-LS2-1. Ecosystems: Interactions, Energy, and Dynamics. Analyze and interpret data to provide evidence for the effects of resource availability on organisms and populations of organisms in an ecosystem.
- MS-LS2-2. Ecosystems: Interactions, Energy, and Dynamics. Construct an explanation that predicts patterns of interactions among organism across multiple ecosystems.
- MS-LS2–4. Ecosystems: Interactions, Energy, and Dynamics. Construct an argument supported by empirical evidence that changes to physical or biological components of an ecosystem affect populations.

Table 4.7 (*continued*)

SCIENCE AND ENGINEERING PRACTICES

Constructing Explanations and Designing Solutions
- Construct an explanation that includes qualitative or quantitative relationships between variables that predict phenomena.

Engaging in Argument from Evidence
- Construct an oral and written argument supported by empirical evidence and scientific reasoning to support or refute an explanation or a model for a phenomenon or a solution to a problem.

Analyzing and Interpreting Data
- Analyze and interpret data to provide evidence for phenomena.

Scientific Knowledge is Based on Empirical Evidence
- Science disciplines share common rules of obtaining and evaluating empirical evidence.

DISCIPLINARY CORE IDEAS

LS2.A: Interdependent Relationships in Ecosystems
- Organisms, and populations of organisms, are dependent on their environmental interactions both with other living things and with nonliving factors.
- In any ecosystem, organisms and populations with similar requirements for food, water, oxygen, or other resources may compete with each other for limited resources, access to which consequently constrains their growth and reproduction.
- Growth of organisms and population increases are limited by access to resources.
- Similarly, predatory interactions may reduce the number of organisms or eliminate whole populations of organisms. Mutually beneficial interactions, in contrast, may become so interdependent that each organism requires the other for survival. Although the species involved in these competitive, predatory, and mutually beneficial interactions vary across ecosystems, the patterns of interactions of organisms with their environments, both living and nonliving, are shared.

LS2.C: Ecosystem Dynamics, Functioning, and Resilience
- Ecosystems are dynamic in nature; their characteristics can vary over time. Disruptions to any physical or biological component of an ecosystem can lead to shifts in all its populations.

CROSSCUTTING CONCEPTS

Patterns
- Patterns can be used to identify cause and effect relationships.

Cause and Effect
- Cause and effect relationships may be used to predict phenomena in natural or designed systems.

Influence of Science, Engineering, and Technology on Society and the Natural World
- All human activity draws on natural resources and has both short and long-term consequences, positive as well as negative, for the health of people and the natural environment.

Stability and Change
- Small changes in one part of a system might cause large changes in another part.

Table 4.7 (*continued*)

Science Addresses Questions About the Natural and Material World
- Scientific knowledge can describe the consequences of actions but does not necessarily prescribe the decisions that society takes.

COMMON CORE STATE STANDARDS FOR MATHEMATICS
MATHEMATICAL PRACTICES
- MP1. Make sense of problems and persevere in solving them.
- MP2. Reason abstractly and quantitatively.
- MP3. Construct viable arguments and critique the reasoning of others.
- MP4. Model with mathematics.
- MP5. Use appropriate tools strategically.
- MP6. Attend to precision.
- MP8. Look for and express regularity in repeated reasoning.

MATHEMATICAL CONTENT
- 7.SP.A.1. Understand that statistics can be used to gain information about a population byexamining a sample of the population; generalizations about a population from a sample are valid only if the sample is representative of that population. Understand that random sampling tends to produce representative samples and support valid inferences.
- 7.SP.A.2. Use data from a random sample to draw inferences about a population with an unknown characteristic of interest. Generate multiple samples (or simulated samples) of the same size to gauge the variation in estimates or predictions. For example, estimate the mean word length in a book by randomly sampling words from the book; predict the winner of a school election based on randomly sampled survey data. Gauge how far off the estimate or prediction might be.
- 7.SP.B.3. Informally assess the degree of visual overlap of two numerical data distributions with similar variabilities, measuring the difference between the centers by expressing it as a multiple of a measure of variability.
- 7.SP.B.4. Use measures of center and measures of variability for numerical data from random samples to draw informal comparative inferences about two populations.

COMMON CORE STATE STANDARDS FOR ENGLISH LANGUAGE ARTS
READING STANDARDS
- RI.7.8. Trace and evaluate the argument and specific claims in a text, assessing whether the reasoning is sound and the evidence is relevant and sufficient to support the claims.
- RI.7.9. Analyze how two or more authors writing about the same topic shape their presentations of key information by emphasizing different evidence or advancing different interpretations of facts.

WRITING STANDARDS
- W.7.1. Write arguments to support claims with clear reasons and relevant evidence.
- W.7.1.a. Introduce claim(s), acknowledge alternate or opposing claims, and organize the reasons and evidence logically.

Table 4.7 (*continued*)

- W.7.1.b. Support claim(s) with logical reasoning and relevant evidence, using accurate, credible sources and demonstrating an understanding of the topic or text.
- W.7.1.c. Use words, phrases, and clauses to create cohesion and clarify the relationships among claim(s), reasons, and evidence.
- W.7.1.e. Provide a concluding statement or section that follows from and supports the argument presented.
- W.7.2. Write informative/explanatory texts to examine a topic and convey ideas, concepts, and information through the selection, organization, and analysis of relevant content.
- W.7.2.a. Introduce a topic clearly, previewing what is to follow; organize ideas, concepts, and information, using strategies such as definition, classification, comparison/contrast, and cause/effect; include formatting (e.g., headings), graphics (e.g., charts, tables), and multimedia when useful to aiding comprehension.
- W.7.2.b. Develop the topic with relevant facts, definitions, concrete details, quotations, or other information and examples.
- W.7.2.d. Use precise language and domain-specific vocabulary to inform about or explain the topic.
- W.7.3.c. Use a variety of transition words, phrases, and clauses to convey sequence and signal shifts from one time frame or setting to another.
- W.7.6. Use technology, including the Internet, to produce and publish writing and link to and cite sources as well as to interact and collaborate with others, including linking to and citing sources.
- W.7.7. Conduct short research projects to answer a question, drawing on several sources and generating additional related, focused questions for further research and investigation.
- W.7.8. Gather relevant information from multiple print and digital sources, using search terms effectively; assess the credibility and accuracy of each source; and quote or paraphrase the data and conclusions of others while avoiding plagiarism and following a standard format for citation.
- W.7.9. Draw evidence from literary or informational texts to support analysis, reflection, and research.

SPEAKING AND LISTENING STANDARDS
- SL.7.1. Engage effectively in a range of collaborative discussions (one-on-one, in groups, and teacher-led) with diverse partners on grade 7 topics, texts, and issues, building on others' ideas and expressing their own clearly.
- SL.7.1.a. Come to discussions prepared, having read or researched material under study; explicitly draw on that preparation by referring to evidence on the topic, text, or issue to probe and reflect on ideas under discussion.
- SL.7.1.b. Follow rules for collegial discussions, track progress toward specific goals and deadlines, and define individual roles as needed.
- SL.7.1.c. Pose questions that elicit elaboration and respond to others' questions and comments with relevant observations and ideas that bring the discussion back on topic as needed.

Table 4.7 (*continued*)

• SL.7.1.d. Acknowledge new information expressed by others and, when warranted, modify their own views. • SL.7.3. Delineate a speaker's argument and specific claims, evaluating the soundness of the reasoning and the relevance and sufficiency of the evidence. • SL.7.4. Present claims and findings, emphasizing salient points in a focused, coherent manner with pertinent descriptions, facts, details, and examples; use appropriate eye contact, adequate volume, and clear pronunciation. • SL.7.5. Include multimedia components and visual displays in presentations to clarify claims and findings and emphasize salient points. *FRAMEWORK FOR 21ST CENTURY LEARNING* • Global Awareness • Environmental Literacy • Civic Literacy • Creativity and Innovation • Critical Thinking and Problem Solving • Communication and Collaboration • Information Literacy • Media Literacy • ICT Literacy

Table 4.8 Key Vocabulary in Lesson 3

Key Vocabulary	Definition
data	facts that are collected and analyzed
generalization	making a statement about a population based on information from a representative sample
inference	drawing a conclusion based on facts and evidence collected
population	the total of all species within a specified area
representative sample	subset of the population whose characteristics reflect those of the entire population
sample	subset of the population
statistics	The practice of collecting and analyzing data for the purpose of making inferences about the whole population based on a representative sample

TEACHER BACKGROUND INFORMATION

Think about the national advertisement that says nine out of ten dentists prefer a particular brand of toothpaste. Where did these numbers come from? In this case the assumed population is all dentists within the United States; however, it is unlikely that the advertisers surveyed every dentist. Instead, the advertisers based their statement on data collected from a sample of dentists and then generalized the finding to the population of dentists.

This lesson will help students make sense of population sampling. It is important to help students understand that populations can vary based on what they are examining. A population is defined as all the individuals or objects with a particular characteristic. Often individuals are interested in answering a question about a particular population. For example, a biologist might be interested in the density of a particular fish species in the local lake. It is not feasible for them to count each and every fish; therefore, they need to develop a strategy for estimating the population through the use of sampling. From this sample, the biologist can make inferences about the population. Limited time and budgets make it impractical to collect data about every individual in a population, so information is collected from a sample of individuals in the population, and this information is used to make inferences about the population. Figure 4.1 provides a visual image that could be used with students to depict this process.

Figure 4.4 Population Sampling

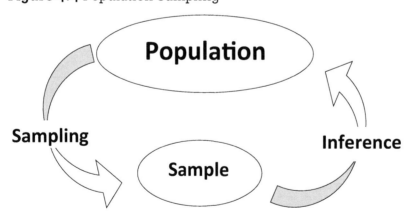

Researchers can use a variety of sampling strategies that can be classified as either probability or non-probability sampling methods. In probability sampling, each individual in the population has a known chance of being in the sample. Examples of probability sampling include random, systematic, or stratified sampling. Any sample that is not random is considered to be non-probability sampling; examples include convenience, purposive, and snowball. For descriptions of these and more information about sampling see the following resources:

- Conjoint.ly, "Research Methods Knowledge Base" at *www.socialresearchmethods. net/kb/sampprob.php*

- OER Commons, "Sampling in Relation to Probability" at *www.oercommons.org/ courseware/lesson/4290/overview*

- Khan Academy, "Sampling Methods Review" at *www.khanacademy.org/math/ statistics-probability/designing-studies/sampling-methods-stats/a/sampling-methods-review*

- Khan Academy, "Random Sampling" at *www.khanacademy.org/test-prep/praxis-math/praxis-math-lessons/gtp--praxis-math--lessons--statistics-and-probability/a/gtp--praxis-math--article--random-sampling--lesson*

The following resources about making inferences based upon data collected from a sample may also be helpful:

- Khan Academy, "Making Inferences from Random Samples" at *www. khanacademy.org/math/cc-seventh-grade-math/cc-7th-probability-statistics/cc-7th-population-sampling/e/making-inferences-from-random-samples*

- Annenberg Learner, "Learning Math: Data Analysis, Statistics, and Probability" at *www.learner.org/series/learning-math-data-analysis-statistics-and-probability/ classroom-case-studies-grades-6-8/inferences-and-predictions-35-minutes/*

COMMON MISCONCEPTIONS

Students will have various types of prior knowledge about the concepts introduced in this lesson. Table 4.9 describes common misconceptions students may have concerning these concepts. Because of the breadth of students' experiences, it is not possible to anticipate every misconception that students may bring as they approach this lesson. Incorrect or inaccurate prior understanding of concepts can influence student learning in the future, however, so it is important to be alert to misconceptions such as those presented in the table.

Table 4.9 Common Misconceptions About the Concepts in Lesson 3

Topic	Student Misconception	Explanation
Equiprobability bias	The tendency to believe that random events are likely to occur with equal probability, or the tendency to believe that all outcomes of an experiment are equally likely (Ang & Sherrill, 2014).	The probability of events is affected by mediating factors; Ang and Sherill (2014) present the example of rolling dice – when two dice are rolled, some sums are more likely than others.

Table 4.9 (*continued*)

Topic	Student Misconception	Explanation
Random sampling	Random means that something is unpredictable or haphazard and therefore a random sample is taken with no planning or forethought (Neuman, 2014).	In mathematical sampling, random sampling means that each unit in a population has an equal chance of being selected for the sample (Neuman, 2014).
Representativeness	The tendency to believe that samples that mirror the characteristics of the population are more common that samples that do not mirror the characteristics of the population (Ang & Sherrill, 2014).	Ang and Sherrill (2014) hold out the example of tossing a coin; in their study, students believed that a series of coin tosses resulting in the coin landing with an equal number of heads and tails face up was more likely than a series of tosses that resulted in mostly heads or mostly tails landing face up. In reality, there is an equal probability for both scenarios.
Statistics	Statistics (for example, 60% of dentists believe that flossing is not necessary) are always representative of the population.	Statistics based on data that are collected from a non-random sample or a sample that did not use good sampling techniques (for example, using a very small sample) may not represent the population.

PREPARATION FOR LESSON 3

Review the Teacher Background Information provided (pp. 102–103), assemble the materials for the lesson, duplicate student handouts, and preview videos included within the Learning Plan Components.

In the next lesson, Lesson 4, students will address the module challenge. One component of the challenge is for student teams to present their challenge solutions to a panel of experts. You should begin to plan now if you wish to invite guests to fill this role. You might wish to invite local government representatives, park rangers, naturalists, biologists, or others to serve as experts. Alternatively, you may wish to invite parents or school administrators to serve as the expert panel. You should issue these invitations early, being sure to stipulate the time commitment required for this task and what the guests will be expected to do (i.e., listen to the presentations and ask students questions).

The focus in this lesson is on probability, sampling, and making inferences. The content spans both science and mathematics and therefore the primary lesson content is presented as content for both science and mathematics classes and is appropriate for either or both content areas.

Data from the US Center for Disease Control (CDC) suggests that only about 9–10% of Americans eat the recommended amount of fruit and vegetables (*www.cdc.gov/nccdphp/dnpao/division-information/media-tools/adults-fruits-vegetables.html*). To prepare before the lesson, you should collect data from your class about how many believe they eat the recommended amounts of fruit and vegetables. Provide students with slips of paper and have them write either "yes" or "no" in answer to the question "Do you eat fruits and vegetables at least four days each week?" Assure students that their responses are confidential and no one will know how they answered. Based on the number of each response, prepare a paper bag with counters for each group of four students; use green counters to represent the number of students who answered "yes" and red counters to represent the students who said "no."

LEARNING PLAN COMPONENTS
Introductory Activity/Engagement

Connection to the Challenge: Begin each day of this lesson by directing students' attention to the module challenge. Remind students that, working in teams, they will determine an appropriate mathematical model to measure the population of their team's assigned species. Hold a brief class discussion each day of how students' learning in the previous days' lessons contributed to their ability to complete the challenge. You may wish to create a class list of key ideas on chart paper.

Mathematics and Science Classes: Tell students that according to the Gallup-Healthways Well-Being Index, 55.1% of Americans frequently consume the recommended amount of fruits and vegetables. (*www.gallup.com/poll/182249/gallup-daily-frequent-produce-consumption.aspx*). Hold a class discussion about this statement asking students the following questions:

- What does this statement mean?

- What questions do you have about this statement?

- Where do you think Gallup found the information to report this?

Tell students that to gather data, the Gallup-Healthways Well-Being Index conducts telephone interviews with approximately 15,000 adults in the US to determine the percentage of Americans who consume the recommended amount of produce. They ask people the following question: "In the last seven days, on how many days did you have five or more servings of fruits and vegetables?" Those who respond with four or more days are described as eating produce frequently.

Next, ask students the following questions:

- What is the US population? (in 2022, about 332,000,000)

- Should we let these 15,000 adults answer for the entire US population?

- Do you think the data that Gallup presented is an accurate estimate of how much produce Americans eat?

- What percentage of the US population provided data for this poll? (about.004%)

Tell students that the Gallup company often takes polls like these using a sample of adults aged 18 and older to make claims. They distribute this information widely and you often hear their polls quoted on the news and in newspapers. Ask students to work in pairs to answer the following question:

- Do you think that we could say from this data that worldwide, more than half of humans are getting the recommended daily amount of fruits and vegetables? Why or why not?

Have student pairs share out what they decided.

Next, ask students the following questions to discuss as a class:

- What percent of our school population frequently eats fruits and vegetables (eating fruits and vegetables at least four days each week)?

- How could we find the answer to this question?

- Would we ask every single student in the school?

- How would our school compare to a school in another state? What about in another country?

Have students work with a partner to answer the following question:

- What is the difference between population and sample?

Have student pairs share their ideas with the class. In the discussion, be sure to ask questions that will lead students to understand that population and sample are context dependent. For example, in a study about US middle school students' eating habits, their school would be a sample (all middle school students in the US is the population), but in a study that is examining the eating habits of your specific school, your class might be the sample (all students in the school would be the population).

Tell students that in this lesson they will learn about sampling from a population and will learn how to count numbers of individuals in a population based on a sample, determine if the sample represents the characteristics of the population, make generalizations, and then make inferences about the population based on the sample.

Give student challenge teams some time to discuss the question below, and then have students each create a STEM Research Notebook entry answering the question:

How could we use the idea of sampling to create a mathematical model to count the population of our group's assigned species?

STEM Research Notebook Entry

Have each student answer the following question in their STEM Research Notebooks: How could our team use the idea of sampling to create a mathematical model to count the population of our group's assigned species?

Activity/Exploration

Science and Mathematics Classes: Show students the PBS LearningMedia video "Random Sampling and Estimation: Lake Victoria" at *www.pbslearningmedia.org/resource/mgbh.math.sp.victoria/random-sampling-and-estimation-lake-victoria/*. The video shows how Kenyan scientists are trying to determine the population of endangered species of fish found in Lake Victoria. Before showing the video, ask students to look for how the scientists (1) use random sampling to make estimates about the fish population and (2) use the collected data to learn about the fish population. After watching the video, hold a class discussion, asking students:

- How did scientists use random sampling to make estimates about the fish population?

- How did scientists use the collected data to learn about the fish population?

- How will these data help the scientists in their efforts to conserve these species?

Next, have students connect this sampling technique to the module challenge in their STEM Research Notebooks.

STEM Research Notebook Entry

Have students answer the following question in their STEM Research Notebooks:

Why did the unique species of fish begin to disappear from Lake Victoria? (Answer: The lake was managed to maximize fishing. New species were introduced, which caused the unique species of fish to disappear.)

What are scientists doing to help preserve the unique species of fish in Lake Victoria? (Answer: They are studying the various populations of fish by trying to find where the fish are located in the lake and taking random samples in order to determine how viable they are.)

How were random samples taken in Mauna Dam? (Answer: On a monthly basis, scientists were catching the fish in a certain area, recording the number caught, and analyzing the data. They divided the area of the entire dam by the area

covered (i.e., where the fish were caught) and estimated the total population by looking at the averages of the samples. Then, they determined what they believed the population to be, based on a margin of error.)

Would the sampling technique the Kenyan scientists used in the video be appropriate to use for your assigned species? Why? Why not?

Class Data – Fruit and Vegetable Consumption

Next, remind students of the Gallup poll about fruits and vegetables. Tell students that they will collect data for students in the class about how many do and do not eat fruits and vegetables at least four days each week (see Preparation for Lesson 3, p. 105). Introduce the idea of a random sample as a sample in which every individual in the population has an equal chance of being selected for the sample. Ask students who the population is in this case (the class). Show students the bags you prepared and explain that green counters represent those students who do eat produce at least four days each week and red are those who do not (see Preparation for Lesson 3, p. 105). Ask students how they can take a random sample of the counters representing students. Students should understand that they will draw counters without looking in the bag. Ask for other ideas (for example, shaking the bag before each drawing to be sure that counters are mixed; being sure that the counters are the same size, shape, and weight).

Have students work in groups of four. Each of the four students should take turns drawing counters out of the bag to create a sample of four counters. Have students record the number of red and green counters drawn in a table in their STEM Research Notebooks (tell them that they will fill out the percentage column later) using a table similar to that in Table 4.10 and then replace all counters in the bag and shake the bag. They should repeat this procedure five times.

Table 4.10 Sample Table for Class Data, Produce Consumption Activity

Number of Students in Class:			
Trial #	Number of Green Counters Drawn	Number of Red Counters Drawn	Percentage of Students Who Eat Produce at Least 4 Days a Week
1			
2			
3			
4			
5			

Next, hold a class discussion about how to calculate the percentage of students who eat the recommended amount of produce (number of green counters/number of students in class). Have students calculate the percentage of green counters (students who eat the recommended amount of produce) for each of the five trials and record that data in the tables in their notebooks.

Next, have each team record their five percentages on a class chart. Discuss the range of percentages and how they compare to the actual percentage of students. Hold a class discussion about why the percentages vary and if the data is a good representation of your class (the population). Ask students for their ideas about how they could represent their five trials in a single piece of data (find an average percentage). Have students calculate the average percentage of students who eat the recommended amount of fruit and vegetables and record the average in their STEM Research Notebooks.

Next, have each group share their average percentage and create a class chart of percentages. Have students create bar graphs (or use an online graphing tool such as the NCES Kids' Zone Create a Graph page at *https://nces.ed.gov/nceskids/createagraph/default.aspx*), and create a graph that can be shared by the class for discussion. Tell students what the actual percentage was and have students draw a red line through the actual percentage on their graphs. See Figure 4.5 for an example.

Figure 4.5 Sample Graph, Produce Consumption Activity

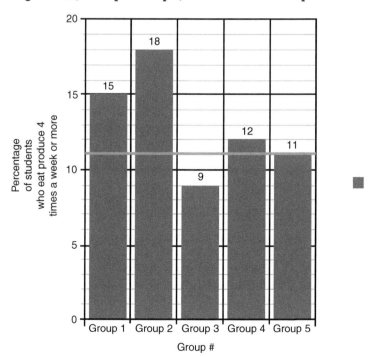

Hold a class discussion about the data, asking the following:

- Did the number of counters drawn vary from sample to sample?

- Why?

- How many of the groups' samples in the bar graph were less than 2% away from the true population percentage?

- How well would your group's sample predict the actual percentage of people in our class who frequently eat fruits and vegetables?

- What is a way to increase your chances of drawing a sample that would allow you to make an estimate that is close to the true population percentage? (If students don't suggest taking a larger sample, you should suggest it.)

Have students create a new table (similar to Table 4.10) in their STEM Research Notebooks and have them repeat the activity, this time having each student in the group draw two counters for a sample size of eight. Have students calculate percentages of green counters and an average percentage for each group. Ask students the following questions:

Did an increase in sample size increase the number of samples that were within 1–2% of the true population percentage? Why? Why not?

STEM Research Notebook Entry

Have students respond to the following questions in their STEM Research Notebooks:

- Describe in your own words what a sample is and how sampling will help you create a mathematical model to count your assigned species population.

- What happens when you choose a larger sample?

- How could you use the sampling technique we used in class to determine the number of members of your species?

Next, remind students of the Gallup poll. Tell them that last year's seventh grade students disagreed with the Gallup poll that indicated 55.1% of the US population eats fruits and vegetables at least four times each week. These students didn't believe the sample was representative. Ask students the following questions:

- What do you think it means for a sample to be representative?

- Do you agree or disagree with the students? Why? Why not?

Last year's students believed that the Gallup survey did not represent their population – US children – because the study only included participants 18 and older. Ask students the following questions:

- Why do you think students felt this way?

- What percent of the US population are under 18 years old? (students will likely not know this although they may make guesses)

- Where could we find data about how many people in the US are under 18? Suggest the U.S. Census Bureau (visit Census Quick Facts at *www.census.gov/ quickfacts/fact/table/US/PST04522*)

- Why would knowing this be important?

- One student suggested that we should conduct a survey at our school to know how many people under 18 in the US eat the recommended amounts of produce. Do you agree or disagree with this student?

- If we were to conduct a study at our school, what question would we really be asking?

Tell students that they will conduct a study to determine the percent of students in the school who frequently eat fruits and vegetables. Have students work in pairs to answer the following questions:

- How will we answer the question about what percent of students in the school eat fruits and vegetables?

- Will we ask the entire school or can we use a sample? Why?

- Do you think our class's data was a good sample of the entire school? Why or why not?

- How will we determine our sample?

- What are some sampling techniques we could use to draw a sample? (for example, randomly choose a class from each grade, randomly choose students from the whole school, ask who wants to participate in the study, have students in our class ask others they know to participate)

Have student pairs share their answers with the entire class.

Sampling Strategy Posters

Tell students that before conducting a survey or study, a researcher needs to know about sampling strategies, or ways to identify a sample from which to collect data. Remind them that they used random sampling in their class produce consumption activity.

Assign each student one of the sampling strategies listed below and have them conduct Internet research and answer the following prompts and questions for the technique they research in their STEM Research Notebooks:

- Describe the sampling strategy.

- In what situations would you use this technique? Why would this technique be the best for these situations?

- What are the benefits of this strategy?

- What are the disadvantages of this strategy?

Sampling strategies:

- Random sampling

- Systematic sampling

- Stratified sampling

- Convenience sampling

- Quota sampling

- Snowball sampling

- Cluster sampling

After students have completed their research, have each student create a poster that shares what they learned about their sampling strategy. Choose one student for each sampling strategy to present their findings and poster to the class, and have students take notes to answer the above questions for each sampling strategy in their STEM Research Notebooks. Post at least one poster for each strategy in the classroom for student reference.

STEM Research Notebook Prompt

Have students respond in their STEM Research Notebooks to the following prompt based upon what they learned from the sampling strategy posters: Which sampling strategy would be best for studying the healthy eating habits of your school. Why?

Design Your Own Produce Consumption Study

Tell students that they are going to design a study that explores if the Gallup poll results for adults are similar to results for the seventh graders at their school. Work as a class to formulate a research question. Make sure students understand that a research question must be clear, must be researchable, must identify the population, and must identify what the researcher is trying to learn. Have students gather into their challenge teams and formulate a research question for researching the produce eating habits of students at their school.

Have each team share its research question and discuss whether it meets the criteria mentioned above. Choose one of the research questions to use for the class, or have the class work together to combine the best elements of multiple questions into a single research question (for example, *What percentage of students eat fruits and vegetables frequently?* is too vague a question, whereas *What percentage of 7th grade students at our school eat fruits and vegetables at least four days each week?* is clear, researchable, identifies a population, and identifies what the researchers are trying to learn).

Next, have student teams discuss each sampling strategy and its appropriateness for the study they are designing, and offer evidence to support the claim of appropriateness. Students should each create a sampling strategy decision table in their STEM Research Notebooks to record their answers (see Table 4.11 for a sample table):

- Which of the sampling strategies would be appropriate for answering the question?

- What evidence supports this claim?

- What would be the best sampling strategy to use to answer this question?

Table 4.11 Sample of Sampling Strategy Decision Table

Sampling Strategy Decision Table		
Sampling Strategy	*Appropriate for this Study?*	*Evidence to Support Claim*
Random sampling		
Systematic sampling		
Stratified sampling		
Convenience sampling		
Quota sampling		
Snowball sampling		
Cluster sampling		
The best type of sampling to use for this study is _____. This is the best type of sampling to use because:		

Discuss the students' responses as a class and assign a sampling technique to each group of two to three students. Using their assigned sampling technique, each group will decide how they will collect their data to help them answer the question. Remind students that if they are going to compare these two studies, they must ask people the same question. Remind them that the question used in the Gallup poll was "In the last seven days, on how many days did you have five or more servings of fruits and vegetables?" Tell students that each team will create a research plan, but the class will choose just one plan to use for the study and that the whole class will use this plan. Students may identify other teams to carry out parts of the study (for example, two teams could collect data, one team could analyze data, one team could prepare a presentation). Students should each record a research plan in their STEM Research Notebooks that includes the following information that their team agrees upon:

- Our research question is: _____

- Our population is (who are they and how many of them are there): _____

- We are using the following sampling strategy: _____

- We want to collect data from this number of people: _____

- This would be _____% of the population.

- This is how we will collect our data (for example, a printed survey that students return, a web-based survey, asking questions and recording the answer):
  _____

- The following people will collect data: _____

- We will collect data on (date or dates): _____

- This is how we will record our data: _____

- After we collect our data, we will analyze it by: _____

- This is who will analyze the data: _____

- We will present our findings by: _____

- This is who will prepare the presentation of findings: _____

After each team has prepared its plan, have teams present their plans to the class and have the class vote on a plan to use.

Students will then work as a class to carry out the study they have designed. Once data has been collected, analyzed, and a presentation has been prepared and presented, hold a class discussion asking the following:

- What are some things you noticed about the data?

- Do you think the sampling strategy used was the best one? Why or why not?

- Was the data similar to the data in the Gallup poll? Why (or why not) do you think this is?

- What are some ways that we could use the findings of this study? (for example, start a campaign in the school to promote eating the recommended amounts of fruit and vegetables)

Connect students' learning about sampling to the module challenge by having them create a STEM Research Notebook entry describing the sampling strategies that would and would not work for the module challenge.

STEM Research Notebook Entry

Have each student create a table in their STEM Research Notebooks to determine which sampling strategies would be appropriate for counting the population of their assigned species (similar to Table 4.11).

After students have completed their notebook entries, discuss as a class which sampling strategies would work for counting the population of teams' assigned species.

ELA Connection: In this connection, students will be learning about inferences from what they read in text. Making inferences is a vital comprehension skill. Help students develop awareness of the process and develop the habit of purposefully reading beyond the literal by teaching them to use this inference algorithm: TEXT INFORMATION + BACKGROUND KNOWLEDGE = INFERENCE. Students can practice this skill, and support their comprehension of the content explored in this module, by using a simple chart that includes the following columns: Important information from the text; What I already know about this; and Inference.

Remind students that "text" may be printed words, graphics, spoken words, visual images, etc. It is also worthwhile to raise student awareness of the importance of activating background knowledge before they read or listen to a text. Teach students to purposefully think, "What do I already know about this topic?" before launching into a new text. Students enjoy and benefit from learning about learning. Consider teaching about schema theory and encouraging students to observe how teachers in various classes activate schema in the lessons they teach.

Social Studies Connection: Discuss how data and inferences have influenced history. For example, introduce students to the 1948 presidential election fiasco in which Gallup predicted that Dewey would win the presidential election. Truman actually won the election; however, the *Chicago Tribune* had already printed that Dewey won the election. Similarly, in 1936 the *Literary Digest*, a respected publication that had correctly predicted the outcome of the previous five elections based upon opinion polls, predicted that Alfred Landon would win the presidential election; Franklin D. Roosevelt won the election with 523 electoral votes while Lanon received only 8. The Talk the Vote website offers information on the Roosevelt vs. Landon presidential election, including a speech from Landon: *http://talkthevote.blogspot.com/2012/10/1936-roosevelt-vs-landon.html.*

Introduce the idea to students that much of what we see in the news is data that researchers have collected from people. Pose the following scenarios to students and ask them if they think that data was collected from a population or using a sample and how they know that:

a) Researchers found that 80% of the novice drivers wandered into the other lane when texting while 60% of experienced drivers wandered into the other lane while texting.

b) Michael Jackson's *Thriller* is the top-selling record (CD/Album) of all time, selling least 51 million copies worldwide.

c) In the 2010 US Census, the US population was 50.8% female and 49.2% male.

Show students a news website such as National Public Radio (*www.npr.org*). Review the headlines and ask students to identify articles that used data based on samples. When you have identified some articles that use data from samples to make inferences about an issue, read the article together, looking for evidence of how the sample was taken. Hold a class discussion about how data is obtained and used for current issues, how to read articles and assess them for credibility in the way data was collected and used, and how to identify credible sources of news (for example, see *https://libguides. ucmerced.edu/news/reputable* and *https://libguides.ucmerced.edu/news/reputable*). Create a class list of practices to identify credible news sites.

Explanation

Science and Mathematics Classes: Students will apply their understanding of sampling to making inferences, explaining how sampling strategies impact their ability to draw inferences and make generalizations.

First, check for understanding of sampling techniques by having students read the following scenario and answer the three questions posed:

Maria and Chris conducted a study to determine what percentage of seventh graders preferred to attend a movie within the first week of its release date. They obtained a database of names of seventh grade mathematics teachers in the state and assigned a unique number to each teacher. Then they used a random number generator to select 20 seventh grade teachers in the state. They emailed a survey out to those 20 teachers asking if they would be willing to ask their students about their movie-going preference. They had a response rate of 40%, which means that only eight teachers responded to the survey. Their survey showed that 60% of seventh grade students preferred to see a new movie within a week of it coming out in theatres.

- What sampling technique did Maria and Chris use?

- Why do you think they chose this technique?

- Is there a sampling technique that would be more appropriate to use to answer this question? Why? Why not?

Next, have students answer individually, then discuss with a partner, and then discuss as a whole class the following question: When you hear the word representative what comes to mind? (You may need to use common contexts such as the House of Representatives to help students make sense of the word.) Next, hold a whole-class discussion asking the following questions:

- What do you think it means for a sample to be representative?

- Is Maria and Chris's sample representative? Why? Why not? What would you do differently?

Introduce the term "generalizable" and discuss what that means with your students. Use the following questions to demonstrate the effect of generalizing:

- If there were 10,000 seventh graders in the state, approximately how many would prefer to watch a movie within a week of it coming out in theatres according to Maria and Chris's study? How do you know?

- If eight teachers responded to the survey, and each of them had 24 students in their class who shared answers to the question, how many students did Maria and Chris collect data from?

- What percentage of the population is this?

- Do you think that it was reasonable to generalize the findings of the study to the population based on responses from this percentage of students? Why or why not?

STEM Research Notebook Entry

Have students respond to the following questions in their STEM Research Notebooks: What does it mean for a sample to be representative? As you devise your mathematical model to measure the population of your species, how can you ensure that your sample is representative and can be used to generalize to your population?

Pose the following scenario to students:

Mr. Fofana's seventh grade class explored GMOs in class last month and the students wanted to find out how many people in their town of 20,000 wanted to have labels on products in their grocery stores stating if they were GMOs. They collected data from a representative random sample of 300 members of the town and found the following data:

Response	Frequency
I want GMO labels on every product.	101
I do not want GMO labels on every product.	100
I don't care.	99

Ask students: What does it mean by "they collected data from a representative random sample"? Tell the students that one of the students, Felicity, believes she can make inferences about the need for labels on every product. Mr. Fofana asks her to describe what she means by an inference. Ask students: If you were Felicity, how would you respond? Present the following conversation between Mr. Fofana, Felicity, and Marcus:

FELICITY: "The data shows that the town does want GMO labeling because it is the most common response."

MARCO: "I disagree with Felicity."

MR. FOFANA: "Why do you disagree with her, Marco?"

MARCO: "Because if we were to plot the data, we would see that they are really close together. There is only one difference between the "Yes" votes and the "No" votes. And, even the "I don't care" votes are really close as well."

Ask students: Do you agree with Felicity, Marco, or neither? Defend your position. Give students time to discuss their findings with their challenge team and discuss whether or not they can make inferences from the data provided.

Next, revisit the data you collected on students' fruit and vegetable consumption. Using their data, have students make inferences about fruit and vegetable consumption for the entire school. Students should compare their results for their school's consumption with the Gallup poll discussed earlier in the lesson.

Elaboration/Application of Knowledge

Mathematics and Science Classes: Have students work in their challenge teams to design a research project in which they must collect data from a small sample and then use that data to estimate the results of a larger population. For example:

- Gather numerical data that has a significant amount of variation, such as the heights or shoe sizes of seventh graders.

- Estimate the mean word length in a book you are reading at school by randomly sampling words from the book.

- Collect data on how many texts middle school students send each day.

Research Plan Activity

Students should submit a plan that describes their study's research questions, how they will conduct the study, how they will ensure that the study sample is representative of the entire population, how many random samples will be taken, and how many data points are in the small sample and the whole population. They will also make a prediction as to what their study will determine.

Have teams of students present their research plan. Review the focus of each study and discuss any questions that teams may have.

Connect the ideas of data analysis and probability by having students use simulations to determine the theoretical and experimental probability of drawing red counters (versus green) out of a jar with a known number of red and green counters. Introduce the law of large numbers that states that when a large number of trials are performed, the average of the results becomes closer to the expected value with successive trials.

Evaluation/Assessment

Students may be assessed on the following performance tasks and other measures listed.

Performance Tasks

Sampling Strategy posters (checklist provided)

Research Plan presentations (checklist provided)

Other Measures

STEM Research Notebook entries

Checklist for Lesson 3 – Sampling Strategy Posters

	Provided	Not Provided
Correctly identified and described the sampling strategies		
Correctly described the benefits of their strategy		
Correctly discussed the drawbacks and limitations to their technique		
Described what contexts this sampling strategy is most effective for		
Provided a justification for their points		
Responded effectively to audience's questions		
Participated in team presentations		

Checklist for Lesson 3 – Research Plan

	Provided	Not Provided
Research questions included and are researchable		
Students described their sampling technique – sampling technique is representative		
Included information on how they will collect data		
Provided information on how they will make generalizations and inferences from the data		
Presented presentation in a clear and coherent manner		
Responded effectively to audience's questions		
Participated in team presentations		

INTERNET RESOURCES

CDC data on fruit and vegetable consumption

- *www.cdc.gov/nccdphp/dnpao/division-information/media-tools/adults-fruits-vegetables. html*

Criteria for credible news sources

- *https://libguides.ucmerced.edu/news/reputable*
- *https://libguides.ucmerced.edu/news/reputable*

Gallup-Healthways Well-Being Index

- *www.gallup.com/poll/182249/gallup-daily-frequent-produce-consumption.aspx*

Making inferences

Khan Academy, "Making Inferences from Random Samples"

- *www.khanacademy.org/math/cc-seventh-grade-math/cc-7th-probability-statistics/cc-7th-population-sampling/e/making-inferences-from-random-samples*

Annenberg Learner, "Learning Math: Data Analysis, Statistics, and Probability"

- *www.learner.org/series/learning-math-data-analysis-statistics-and-probability/classroom-case-studies-grades-6-8/inferences-and-predictions-35-minutes/*

National Public Radio news

- *www.npr.org*

NCES Kids' Zone, "Create a Graph"

- *https://nces.ed.gov/nceskids/createagraph/default.aspx*

PBS LearningMedia video, "Random Sampling and Estimation: Lake Victoria"

- *www.pbslearningmedia.org/resource/mgbh.math.sp.victoria/random-sampling-and-estimation-lake-victoria/*

Sampling information

    Conjoint.ly, "Research Methods Knowledge Base"

- *www.socialresearchmethods.net/kb/sampprob.php*

OER Commons, "Sampling in Relation to Probability"

- *www.oercommons.org/courseware/lesson/4290/overview*

Khan Academy, "Sampling Methods Review"

- *www.khanacademy.org/math/statistics-probability/designing-studies/sampling-methods-stats/a/sampling-methods-review*

Khan Academy, "Random Sampling"

- *www.khanacademy.org/test-prep/praxis-math/praxis-math-lessons/gtp--praxis-math-lessons--statistics-and-probability/a/gtp--praxis-math--article--random-sampling--lesson*

US Census Bureau Quick Facts

- *www.census.gov/quickfacts/fact/table/US/PST04522*

REFERENCES

Ang, L. H., & Shahrill, M. (2014). Identifying students' specific misconceptions in learning probability. *International Journal of Probability and Statistics*, 3(2), 23–29.

Neuman, W. L. (2014). *Social research methods: Qualitative and quantitative approaches.* Pearson.

Lesson Plan 4:
Exploring, Understanding, and Developing Mathematical Models to Estimate Population Totals

In this lesson, students will explore a variety of mathematical models for counting and estimating population totals in a variety of species. They will use the knowledge obtained in the module to develop their own mathematical model for counting their assigned species and present their model to a panel of experts.

ESSENTIAL QUESTIONS

- What are some common models for counting population totals for different species?

- What are some advantages and disadvantages of using this model in the field for a variety of species?

- What is an appropriate mathematical model for counting students' specific assigned species?

- Do the student groups' mathematical model provide effective estimates of their assigned species?

ESTABLISHED GOALS AND OBJECTIVES

At the conclusion of this lesson, students will be able to do the following:

- Identify an invasive species and identify population implications for other species associated with the presence of invasive species in an area

- Identify and apply common mathematical models for counting populations

- Identify advantages and disadvantages of each model for a variety of species

- Create a mathematical model that will provide an accurate estimate of the population of a species

- Present information about population density and models to estimate population density

TIME REQUIRED

Approximately 8 days (approximately 45 minutes each day; see Tables 3.9–3.10, p. 43)

MATERIALS

Required Materials for Lesson 4

- STEM Research Notebooks

- Computers, laptops, tablets, or smartphones (with Internet capability) to conduct Internet research

- Chart paper or poster board (1 per team)

- Red beans for Mark-Recapture activity (600 per team of 4 students)

- White beans for Mark-Recapture activity (200 per team of 4 students)

- Buckets or large plastic containers for Mark-Recapture activity – about 1 gallon size (1 per team of 4 students)

- Three-ounce cups for Mark-Recapture activity (1 per team of 4 students)

- Three-ounce cups for Grid Sampling activity (1 per student)

- Construction paper for Grid Sampling activity (1 per student)

- Rulers (1 per student)

- Scissors (1 per student)

- Markers (1 set per team of 4 students)

- 1 large bag of rice (1 per class)

- Plastic spoons (1 per student)

- Heavy-duty string (for example, cotton twine or jute) (enough to stretch from one side of your classroom to the other)

- Masking tape (1 per class)

- Meter stick (1 per class)

- Module Challenge Criteria handout (1 per student)
- Module Challenge Presentation rubric (1 per student)

SAFETY NOTES

1. Caution students not to eat materials used for activities.

2. Students should use caution when handling scissors, as the sharp points and blades can cut or puncture skin.

3. Have students wash hands with soap and water after activities are completed.

CONTENT STANDARDS AND KEY VOCABULARY

Table 4.12 lists the content standards from the *Next Generation Science Standards* (*NGSS*), *Common Core State Standards* (*CCSS*), and the Framework for 21st Century Learning that this lesson addresses, and Table 4.13 (p. 128) presents the key vocabulary. Vocabulary terms are provided for both teacher and student use. Teachers may choose to introduce some or all of the terms to students.

Table 4.12 Content Standards Addressed in STEM Road Map Module Lesson 4

NEXT GENERATION SCIENCE STANDARDS

PERFORMANCE OBJECTIVES

- MS-LS2-1. Ecosystems: Interactions, Energy, and Dynamics. Analyze and interpret data to provide evidence for the effects of resource availability on organisms and populations of organisms in an ecosystem.
- MS-LS2-2. Ecosystems: Interactions, Energy, and Dynamics. Construct an explanation thatpredicts patterns of interactions among organism across multiple ecosystems.
- MS-LS2–4. Ecosystems: Interactions, Energy, and Dynamics. Construct an argument supported by empirical evidence that changes to physical or biological components of an ecosystem affect populations.

SCIENCE AND ENGINEERING PRACTICES

Constructing Explanations and Designing Solutions

- Construct an explanation that includes qualitative or quantitative relationships between variables that predict phenomena.

Table 4.12 (*continued*)

Engaging in Argument from Evidence
- Construct an oral and written argument supported by empirical evidence and scientific reasoning to support or refute an explanation or a model for a phenomenon or a solution to a problem.

Analyzing and Interpreting Data
- Analyze and interpret data to provide evidence for phenomena.

Scientific Knowledge is Based on Empirical Evidence
- Science disciplines share common rules of obtaining and evaluating empirical evidence.

DISCIPLINARY CORE IDEAS

LS2.A: Interdependent Relationships in Ecosystems
- Organisms, and populations of organisms, are dependent on their environmental interactions both with other living things and with nonliving factors.
- In any ecosystem, organisms and populations with similar requirements for food, water, oxygen, or other resources may compete with each other for limited resources, access to which consequently constrains their growth and reproduction.
- Growth of organisms and population increases are limited by access to resources.
- Similarly, predatory interactions may reduce the number of organisms or eliminate whole populations of organisms. Mutually beneficial interactions, in contrast, may become so interdependent that each organism requires the other for survival. Although the species involved in these competitive, predatory, and mutually beneficial interactions vary across ecosystems, the patterns of interactions of organisms with their environments, both living and nonliving, are shared.

LS2.C: Ecosystem Dynamics, Functioning, and Resilience
- Ecosystems are dynamic in nature; their characteristics can vary over time. Disruptions to any physical or biological component of an ecosystem can lead to shifts in all its populations.

CROSSCUTTING CONCEPTS

Patterns
- Patterns can be used to identify cause and effect relationships.

Cause and Effect
- Cause and effect relationships may be used to predict phenomena in natural or designed systems.

Stability and Change
- Small changes in one part of a system might cause large changes in another part.

COMMON CORE STATE STANDARDS FOR MATHEMATICS

MATHEMATICAL PRACTICES
- MP1. Make sense of problems and persevere in solving them.
- MP2. Reason abstractly and quantitatively.
- MP3. Construct viable arguments and critique the reasoning of others.
- MP4. Model with mathematics.
- MP5. Use appropriate tools strategically.
- MP6. Attend to precision.

Table 4.12 (*continued*)

MATHEMATICAL CONTENT

- 7.SP.A.1. Understand that statistics can be used to gain information about a population by examining a sample of the population; generalizations about a population from a sample are valid only if the sample is representative of that population. Understand that random sampling tends to produce representative samples and support valid inferences.
- 7.SP.A.2. Use data from a random sample to draw inferences about a population with an unknown characteristic of interest. Generate multiple samples (or simulated samples) of the same size to gauge the variation in estimates or predictions. For example, estimate the mean word length in a book by randomly sampling words from the book; predict the winner of a school election based on randomly sampled survey data. Gauge how far off the estimate or prediction might be.

COMMON CORE STATE STANDARDS FOR ENGLISH LANGUAGE ARTS

READING STANDARDS

- RI.7.8. Trace and evaluate the argument and specific claims in a text, assessing whether the reasoning is sound and the evidence is relevant and sufficient to support the claims.
- RI.7.9. Analyze how two or more authors writing about the same topic shape their presentations of key information by emphasizing different evidence or advancing different interpretations of facts.

WRITING STANDARDS

- W.7.1. Write arguments to support claims with clear reasons and relevant evidence.
- W.7.1.a. Introduce claim(s), acknowledge alternate or opposing claims, and organize the reasons and evidence logically.
- W.7.1.b. Support claim(s) with logical reasoning and relevant evidence, using accurate, credible sources and demonstrating an understanding of the topic or text.
- W.7.1.c. Use words, phrases, and clauses to create cohesion and clarify the relationships among claim(s), reasons, and evidence.
- W.7.1.e. Provide a concluding statement or section that follows from and supports the argument presented.
- W.7.2. Write informative/explanatory texts to examine a topic and convey ideas, concepts, and information through the selection, organization, and analysis of relevant content.
- W.7.2.a. Introduce a topic clearly, previewing what is to follow; organize ideas, concepts, and information, using strategies such as definition, classification, comparison/contrast, and cause/effect; include formatting (e.g., headings), graphics (e.g., charts, tables), and multimedia when useful to aiding comprehension.
- W.7.2.b. Develop the topic with relevant facts, definitions, concrete details, quotations, or other information and examples.
- W.7.2.d. Use precise language and domain-specific vocabulary to inform about or explain the topic.
- W.7.3.c. Use a variety of transition words, phrases, and clauses to convey sequence and signal shifts from one time frame or setting to another

---

Table 4.12 (*continued*)

- W.7.6. Use technology, including the Internet, to produce and publish writing and link to and cite sources as well as to interact and collaborate with others, including linking to and citing sources.
- W.7.7. Conduct short research projects to answer a question, drawing on several sources and generating additional related, focused questions for further research and investigation.
- W.7.8. Gather relevant information from multiple print and digital sources, using search terms effectively; assess the credibility and accuracy of each source; and quote or paraphrase the data and conclusions of others while avoiding plagiarism and following a standard format for citation.
- W.7.9. Draw evidence from literary or informational texts to support analysis, reflection, and research.

SPEAKING AND LISTENING STANDARDS
- SL.7.1. Engage effectively in a range of collaborative discussions (one-on-one, in groups, and teacher-led) with diverse partners on grade 7 topics, texts, and issues, building on others' ideas and expressing their own clearly.
- SL.7.1.a. Come to discussions prepared, having read or researched material under study; explicitly draw on that preparation by referring to evidence on the topic, text, or issue to probe and reflect on ideas under discussion.
- SL.7.1.b. Follow rules for collegial discussions, track progress toward specific goals and deadlines, and define individual roles as needed.
- SL.7.1.c. Pose questions that elicit elaboration and respond to others' questions and comments with relevant observations and ideas that bring the discussion back on topic as needed.
- SL.7.1.d. Acknowledge new information expressed by others and, when warranted, modify their own views.
- SL.7.3. Delineate a speaker's argument and specific claims, evaluating the soundness of the reasoning and the relevance and sufficiency of the evidence.
- SL.7.4. Present claims and findings, emphasizing salient points in a focused, coherent manner with pertinent descriptions, facts, details, and examples; use appropriate eye contact, adequate volume, and clear pronunciation.
- SL.7.5. Include multimedia components and visual displays in presentations to clarify claims and findings and emphasize salient points.

FRAMEWORK FOR 21ST CENTURY LEARNING
- Global Awareness
- Environmental Literacy
- Civic Literacy
- Creativity and Innovation
- Critical Thinking and Problem Solving
- Communication and Collaboration
- Information Literacy
- Media Literacy
- ICT Literacy

Table 4.13 Key Vocabulary in Lesson 4

Key Vocabulary	Definition
grid sampling	sampling technique where the sampling area is split into a grid pattern and then random grid areas are chosen to count all the species in the area; those areas are used to estimate the entire population
mark-recapture sampling	sampling strategy where a portion of the population is captured, marked, and released back into the population; then later a sample is taken from the population, and based on the proportion of the sample that is marked an estimate of the size of the population can be made
mathematical model	a method of simulating a real situation using a mathematical technique
population	the total of all species within a specified area
proportion	a portion or part of the population in relation to the whole population
sample	subset of the population
transect sampling	sampling technique where the observer moves along a set path and counts the occurrence of that species as well as the distance the species is from the path

TEACHER BACKGROUND INFORMATION

It will be helpful for you and your students to understand the background of the US Census. More information can be found here: *www.census.gov/history/pdf/cff4.pdf* and activities based on the US Census can be found at *www.census.gov/programs-surveys/ sis/2020census/2020-resources/k-12.html*.

While the US Census counts every human in the country every ten years, this technique may not be possible when trying to find the population of different species on Earth. There are many sampling techniques that scientists use to count populations; however, students will concentrate on mark-recapture, grid sampling, and transect methods in this lesson. The following websites provide information on techniques used to count animal populations:

- *www.geographynotes.com/wildlife-census/how-to-conduct-wildlife-census-3-methods-geography/5963*

- *https://open.oregonstate.education/monitoring/chapter/field-techniques-for-population-sampling-and-estimation/*

- *http://scientistatwork.blogs.nytimes.com/2011/05/03/three-ways-to-count-whales/?_r=0*

- *https://cires.colorado.edu/outreach/sites/default/files/2021-01/Population%20 Estimates%20Teacher%20Guide.pdf*

- *https://adfg.alaska.gov/index.cfm?adfg=wildlifenews.view_article&articles_id=814*

COMMON MISCONCEPTIONS

No new common misconceptions are introduced for this lesson. Instead, we recommend that you review the potential student misconceptions introduced in previous lessons and stay alert to these as students complete their work on the module challenge.

PREPARATION FOR LESSON 4

Review the Teacher Background Information provided, assemble the materials for the lesson, make copies of the student handouts, and preview the video and websites recommended in the Learning Plan Components section that follows.

As in Lesson 3, the content of this lesson spans both science and mathematics and therefore the primary lesson content is presented as content for both science and mathematics classes and is appropriate for either or both content areas.

Students will address the module challenge in this lesson, including having student teams present their challenge solutions to a panel of experts. You should confirm times and expectations with invited guests, and provide them with a copy of the criteria for the module challenge (pp. 138–139). Also, be sure to stipulate the time commitment required for this task and what the guests will be expected to do (i.e., listen to the presentations and ask students questions).

You will need to be prepared to assign student teams each a species that is a nonnative invasive species in your state. Information on these species can be found at the following websites:

- National Invasive Species Information Center – *www.invasivespeciesinfo.gov/unitedstates/state.shtml*

- Exotic Pest Detection by State – *http://pest.ceris.purdue.edu/states.php*

- USGS: Nonindigenous Aquatic Species –*http://nas.er.usgs.gov/queries/StateSearch.aspx*

- USDA: State Noxious Weed Lists –*www.ams.usda.gov/sites/default/files/media/StateNoxiousWeedsSeedList.pdf*

Prepare premade buckets or containers of 600 red beans to simulate the fish in the lake for the Mark-Recapture activity. In a quart-size plastic bag or container have 200 white beans to simulate tagged fish.

For the Grid Sampling activity, prepare three-ounce cups, each with a plastic spoonful of rice in it. Students will measure a leveled spoonful of rice for this activity, so they should have at least this amount in their cup.

For the Transect activity, measure a length of string the length of your classroom or, if you are able to conduct the activity outdoors, around 50–60 feet. Mark the string at regular intervals (for example, every three feet), using masking tape. An option for this activity is to conduct it in an outdoor grassy setting or field. If you are conducting

the activity in the classroom, be prepared to stretch the string from one side of the classroom to the other, making sure that there are objects under and near the string for students to observe (for example, stretch the string across desks and areas of the classroom where there are various objects).

LEARNING PLAN COMPONENTS
Introductory Activity/Engagement

Connection to the Challenge: Begin each day of this lesson by directing students' attention to the module challenge. Remind students that, working in teams, they will determine an appropriate mathematical model to measure the population of their team's assigned species. Hold a brief class discussion each day of how students' learning in the previous days' lessons contributed to their ability to complete the challenge. You may wish to create a class list of key ideas on chart paper.

Science Class: Introduce the concept of non-native invasive species. Show students a video about invasive species such as the National Geographic's "Invasive Species 101" at *www.youtube.com/watch?v=gYNAtw1c7hI*. Before showing the video, tell students to watch for the following, taking notes in their STEM Research Notebooks:

- A definition of invasive species

- Examples of invasive species

- How invasive species are introduced to an area

- What type of problems invasive species can create

- How the spread of invasive species can be limited

After viewing the video, hold a class discussion, asking students to share what they learned about the above topics.

Mathematics Class: Remind students that throughout the module they have been using US Census data.

Access the Census "Quick Facts" site *at www.census.gov/quickfacts*. Have students examine the data in the table and ask students what they think are some interesting facts listed in the table that they have not yet explored. For example, students might note that Internet access data, female ownership of businesses, and mean travel time to work are included in the table. Pose the following problem and have students work in pairs to find a solution, recording their answers in their STEM Research Notebooks:

- What percentage of firms did women own in the most recent census year?

- How many employer firms were there in the US in that year?

- How many firms were owned by women?

Have each team share their answers with the class and review the calculations needed to solve this problem.

Social Studies Connection: Ask students to consider why we collect census data in the US and share their answers with the class. Have the students research the reasons why the US Constitution enables lawmakers to require a census. Bring the students back together and have them share their findings in response to the following questions:

- Does the US Census use population characteristics or sampling statistics?

- Why do we need a total population count of the people in the US?

ELA Connection: N.A.

Activity/Exploration

Science and Mathematics Classes: Students will move through a series of activities culminating in having student teams address the module challenge.

Invasive Species Research

Show students the video "Wild Marlborough – Asian Long Horned Beetles" at *www.youtube.com/watch?t=168&v=ERC4m90cxjU*. Tell students that they will study an invasive species in their home state. Working in their challenge teams, students will research an invasive species in their state. Assign each group one invasive species (see Preparation for Lesson 4, p. 129).

Students will work in their challenge teams to prepare a multimedia presentation, a poster presentation, or a written report on their assigned species. Students should include the following in their report or presentation:

- Common name of the species

- Scientific name of the species

- Native location of the species

- Where and how it became invasive

- How the species affects the natural ecosystem

- What are economic and/or social impacts

- What control measures are possible

Have students present their research findings on the invasive species to the class.

Explain to students that they will be exploring counting models for populations. Have each challenge team use the Internet to explore mark-recapture, grid sampling, and transect counting models. Each student should record answers to the following questions in their STEM Research Notebooks:

- What are advantages and disadvantages of each method?

- Why would you use each method?

Adrienne Redmond-Sanogo et al.

Optional: Have groups create posters of the population counting models to display around the room.

Mark-Recapture Activity[1]

Present the following scenario to students:

A local fish biologist was dispatched to a local lake because of complaints from local fisherman that they were not having any luck catching bass. In order to be able to count the number of fish in the lake, the biologist decided to use the mark-recapture strategy. You will simulate the work of the fish biologist and use mark-recapture to estimate the number of bass (beans) in a lake (the bucket). You will then write a post that can be shared on the lake's social media website.

Give each challenge team a premade bucket of 600 red beans to simulate the fish in the lake (see Preparation for Lesson 4, p. 129) and a plastic bag or container containing 200 white beans to simulate tagged fish. Be sure not to tell the students how many "fish" are in the bucket. Ask students to make estimates of how many "fish" are in the lake (red beans). Record student estimates. Next, say the following:

This morning I went out and caught 200 fish and sent them to be tagged at the fish-tagging station. The fish were tagged and are in this container (pointing to the bag of white beans). We are now going to release them back into the lake.

Have students pour the tagged fish into the bucket to simulate releasing the fish back into the lake.

Ask students to respond as a class to the following questions:

- What would we call our tagged fish? (Scientists refer to this as an initial sample or tagging sample.)

- What would we call all the fish in the lake?

Tell students that in real research, the fish biologists would allow time for the fish to mix with the rest of the fish in the lake; have each team mix the beans together well.

Next, give each team one three-ounce paper cup to serve as a net. Using the cup, have students capture a sample of fish. Tell students that this is their recapture sample. Ask students the following questions:

- How many tagged fish are in the sample?

- How many untagged fish are in the sample?

- How many total fish are in our recaptured sample?

- How can we express the number of tagged fish in our recapture sample as a proportion?

1 This activity was adapted from Morita, J. G. (1999). Capture and recapture your students' interest in statistics. *Mathematics Teaching in the Middle School*, 4(6), 412–418.

Have students simplify the proportion if possible. Next, have students each prepare a table in their STEM Research Notebooks similar to the one in Table 4.14 and record their findings from this first trial in the table.

Table 4.14 Sample Data Table for Mark-Recapture Activity

Trial Number	Number of White Beans Drawn (Marked Fish)	Number of Red Beans Drawn (Unmarked Fish)	Proportion of White Beans to Red Beans (Marked to Unmarked Fish)
1			
2			
3			
4			
5			
6			
7			
8			
9			
10			

Next, tell students to return the sample back into the lake. Have students again mix up the fish (beans) and take another sample using the cup. Ask each group to draw nine more samples, counting and recording the number of tagged fish each time. Have students write their results as a simplified proportion each time. Now ask students the following questions:

- How could we use this information to estimate the number of fish in the lake?

- What assumptions can we make about our sample?

Tell students that, working with their groups, they should use the data they collected to determine the total number of fish in the lake without counting the total fish population in the lake.

Have student groups work for a few minutes to determine how they could use this information to estimate the population. If students struggle with getting started, you can remind them of their experiences with ratios and proportions, and prompt them to think about how they could write this problem as a proportion. For example, students could write the proportion as follows.

$$\frac{\text{\# of tagged fish in sample}}{\text{total \# of fish in sample}} = \frac{\text{number of tagged fish in population}}{\text{total \# of fish in population}}$$

Ask students to think about which trials they would use to find the population, and prompt them to use all trials by finding averages.

Have students share their conclusions for the number of fish in the population, and end the activity by telling students the actual number of fish and discussing how teams' findings compared with the actual value. Wrap up the class discussion about how scientists could use this to estimate the population of other animals such as birds and bears.

- What assumptions does this method rely upon to be accurate?

- What are the limitations of this method?

- How could you use this method to determine the population of your assigned species?

- What effect could this method have on real animals?

An optional extension for this activity is to have students graph total class results and make conjectures about the data.

Have students create a STEM Research Notebook entry in which they connect the mark-recapture method to the challenge.

STEM Research Notebook Entry

Have students respond to the following questions in their STEM Research Notebooks:

- Could you use the mark-recapture technique to estimate the population of your species? Why or why not?

- What difficulties might you encounter in marking members of your species?

- What difficulties might you encounter in recapturing members of your species?

Grid Sampling Activity[2]

Present the following scenario to students:

We are biologists in the field and there have been concerns that the fire ant population is out of control. We will conduct a simulation of the grid method to explore how biologists use this method to count populations in the field.

2 This activity was adapted from NSTA's "How Many Grasshoppers Activity"

Have each student create a 4″ × 4.5″ array on a sheet of construction paper, using rulers and markers to create straight lines (this should divide the construction paper into six equally sized sections). Have students label the grids with the numbers one through six.

Tell students that rice will represent the fire ant population, the construction paper will represent the fire ants' habitat, and the grids on the construction paper represent the sampling areas for the activity. Have each student prepare a data collection table in their STEM Research Notebooks similar to the table in Table 4.15. Next, have students calculate the area of the construction paper and the area of each of the squares they created and record that data in the table.

Table 4.15 Sample Data Collection Table for Grid Sampling Activity

Area of construction paper: _____ Area of each square: _____	
Square Number	Number of Ants (Grains of Rice)
Mean Number of Ants: _____	

Distribute a cup of rice and a plastic spoon to each student. Show students how to fill the plastic spoon and level it. Using this method, have students measure one spoonful of rice and scatter the rice as evenly as possible over the entire construction paper. Next, have students count the number of rice grains in one of the squares and record that data in the table. Students should then count the number of grains of rice in two other squares and record it in their tables. Have students find the mean number of rice grains in the three squares. Then students will multiply the mean by the number of squares to find the approximate number of fire ants in the population.

Ask students questions such as the following:

- How would we determine an estimate for the number of ants in each square? If students don't suggest the mean, you could mention measures of central tendency and ask which would be the most appropriate here.

- If the mean tells us approximately how many fire ants are in one square, how would we find out how many are in the entire grid? If students can't tell you,

you might ask: How many squares are in the grid? How many ants are in each square?

- What is the population density of these fire ants? Prompt students to consider the average number of grains of rice per square; tell students that if they know the number of individuals who are in a specific area, this is the density for that area.

- Did you get the same answer as your peers? Why? Why not?

- Have students count the rice in the three uncounted squares and record the number for the total population in their notebooks. Ask: How close was your estimate based on the three squares you measured to your actual population?

- If there were twice as many fire ants this year as there were last year, how would you respond to the community's concern about the growing population of fire ants?

STEM Research Notebook Entry

In their STEM Research Notebooks, have students answer the following questions:

- What are some limitations and advantages of using the grid model to count a population?

- Would this method work for your assigned species?

Transect Method Activity

Remind students that they have explored mark-recapture methods and grid methods for estimating populations. Tell them that they are now going to explore the use of transects to count populations. A transect is a line stretched over an area of interest. The line needs to have regular increments marked off and it must be held straight and immobile. An option for this activity is to conduct it outdoors in a grassy area. Directions are given here for conducting the activity in the classroom.

Have two students stand at opposite ends of the classroom. Give one end of the string to one student and the other end to the student at the opposite side of the classroom. Tell the students to hold the string taut and immobile.

Holding a meter stick, walk along the path of the string. Stop at each marked-off interval and hold the meter stick perpendicular to the string above the marked spot with the midpoint of the meter stick at the line and have students describe everything they see under the meter stick. Tell students that part of the line transect method is to decide how far on either side of the line an object can be to be included in the count.

In this case, therefore, you are observing items about half a meter on either side of the line. Have students record in their STEM Research Notebooks the length of the transect line, the intervals at which the line is marked, the area of observation (½ meter on either side of the line), and what they observe in the observation area at each marked point. After you have traveled across the entire classroom, ask students what they noticed, asking the following questions:

- If we were to describe only what was underneath the meter stick, would this provide a good description of our classroom? Why? Why not?

- What could we do to get a more accurate picture of our classroom?

If students don't suggest setting up several transect line, suggest it to students.

STEM Research Notebook Entry

Have students respond to the following questions in their STEM Research Notebooks:

- What are some limitations and advantages of using the transect model to count the population?

- Would this method work for your assigned species? Why? Why not?

Module Challenge

Remind students that they have had an opportunity to learn about several mathematical models for counting populations. Ask students to name the population counting models they learned about.

Next, remind students about the module challenge in which they will answer the following question: What is an appropriate mathematical model to measure the population of an identified species on Earth? In this challenge they will work with their teams to devise a model for counting the population of their species and develop a formal presentation of the model for consideration by a panel of experts.

Tell students that they have had an opportunity to think about aspects of this challenge throughout the module. Remind them to refer to their notes in their STEM Research Notebooks and the posters they created in previous lessons. Tell students how much time they will have to create their challenge solutions and create presentations of their solutions. Hand out the Module Challenge rubric attached at the end of this lesson plan and review the rubric as a class. Provide students with the handout outlining the criteria for their challenge solutions and presentations and review the criteria as a class.

Adrienne Redmond-Sanogo et al.

POPULATION COUNTING CHALLENGE CRITERIA

You have been challenged to answer the following question for your team's assigned species:

What is an appropriate mathematical model to measure the population of an identified species on Earth?

In this challenge you will work with your teams to devise a model for counting the population of your species and develop a presentation for consideration by a panel of experts.

Your team's challenge solution and presentation must meet the following criteria:

1. Teams must each pose a research question that is researchable, clear, and identifies the population being studied (e.g., How many green newts are in the public park in Our County, Illinois?)

2. Teams must provide background information including:

   a. how population information could be used

   b. a description of their species' habitat

   c. a description of their species' position in the food chain

   d. threats to their species

3. Teams must clearly define their population, including where they would conduct their population sampling (e.g., the population is the green newts in the public park in Our County, Illinois; or the population is the large mouthed bass in Fish Lake in Anytown, Florida).

(continued)

STUDENT HANDOUT

POPULATION COUNTING CHALLENGE CRITERIA

4. Teams must create a plan for making a reasonable estimate of the population, using one or more of the population counting methods discussed in the module. Teams' plans must include the following:

   a. an explanation of the type of sampling used

   b. a list of materials that would be necessary to carry out the plan

   c. an explanation of how samples will be counted (procedure)

   d. a description of how data will be analyzed (presentation of the mathematical model to determine population size)

5. Teams must create an explanation of how they could use their sample and population estimate to calculate population density.

6. Teams must create a presentation that includes all of the above items. All team members should take part in creating the plan and making the presentation.

You may wish to scaffold team work by having teams decide on roles for each team member before they begin their work. For example, one student might be assigned the role of recording notes from team discussions; one student might be assigned the role of team manager, making sure that the team stays on task and addresses each area of criteria; one student might be assigned the role of creative director, assembling artwork and pictures for the presentation.

Social Studies Connection: Show students a video about issues with global overpopulation, such as the National Geographic's "7 Billion" at *www.youtube.com/watch?v=sc4HxPxNrZ0*. Hold a class discussion about the issues associated with a growing world population.

See Population Education's website "World of 7 Billion" at *www.worldof7billion.org/teacher-resources/middle-school-activities/* for interactive activities for middle school students related to global population.

ELA Connection: The Scientist in the Field series of books (*www.sciencemeetsadventure.com/books/*) features scientists in a wide range of specializations at work in the field. Quite a few of these books show the world of scientists who are dedicated to the understanding and protection of animal populations in the wild. Not only do a number of these books provide readers with an up-close look at many of the procedures addressed above, but they may also serve as valuable mentor texts for nonfiction writers. Using these books in nonfiction reading and writing workshops extends the content area learning and provides a context for growing readers and writers. Consider a project in which students apply their growing knowledge of nonfiction writing conventions to produce books about their assigned species to share with the rest of the school or another authentic audience.

Connecting to the Challenge: Describe the type of scientist that typically studies your assigned species. In your description, provide a sample daily log that would explain what they would be doing in the field.

Explanation

Science and Mathematics Classes: Students will explain what they have learned in the module in their presentations to the panel of experts you assembled. Hold a class discussion about practices for making a professional presentation, asking students for their ideas about what is important in making presentations (for example, speak clearly, dress professionally, make eye contact with the audience, be prepared and organized).

Have students complete a final STEM Research Notebook entry in which they summarize and reflect on their learning from the module.

STEM Research Notebook Entry

Have students respond to the following prompt in their STEM Research Notebooks:

Think ahead to the future: how might you be able to use what you have learned in this module about population sampling, population density, sampling techniques, developing mathematical models, and counting populations?

Social Studies Connection: N.A.

ELA Connection: N.A.

Elaboration/Application of Knowledge

Science and Mathematics Classes: Have student teams discuss the feedback they received from their presentations. Have each team share with the class what they believe were the strong parts of their challenge solutions and presentations and what areas could be improved and how they would improve those elements.

Have students explore careers associated with population growth including, for example, data analysts, demographic researchers, biologists, supply chain and logistics careers, agriculturists, and public health workers.

Social Studies Connection: Explore population growth from the perspectives of the various issues associated with it (e.g., depletion of natural resources, food shortages, and the potential effects of climate change on population distributions). Have students conduct research on issues and possible solutions using websites such as the following:

- "Understanding Global Change" at *https://ugc.berkeley.edu/background-content/population-growth/.*

- United Nations, "Population Growth, Environmental Degradation and Climate Change" at *www.un.org/en/desa/population-growth-environmental-degradation-and-climate-change.*

Have students choose one issue and create an innovative solution to mitigate the issue. Have students create a poster or media presentation presenting the issue they researched and their proposed solution.

ELA Connection: If guests visited to serve as experts for students' challenge presentations, have students write thank you notes.

Evaluation/Assessment

Students may be assessed on the following performance tasks and other measures listed.
Performance Tasks

- Invasive Species research presentation

- Population Counting Model research (posters optional)

- Mark-Recapture activity
- Grid Sampling activity
- Transect activity
- Module Challenge (rubric attached)

Other Measures

- STEM Research Notebook entries

- Participation in class discussions

MODULE CHALLENGE PRESENTATION RUBRIC

	Below Mastery	Approaching Mastery	At Mastery	Comments
Explanation of Population Counting Models	Uses too few, inappropriate, or irrelevant descriptions, facts, details, or examples to support ideas	Uses some descriptions, facts, details, and examples that support ideas, but there may not be enough, or some are irrelevant	Uses relevant, well-chosen descriptions, facts, details, and examples to support claims, findings, arguments, or an answer to describe the population counting models	
Organization of Presentation	Does not include two or more required criteria Does not have a main idea or presents ideas in an order that does not make sense Does not have an introduction and/or conclusion	Includes most criteria, but may be missing one There is a flow of ideas, but some ideas may be presented in the wrong order Has an introduction and conclusion, but they may not be effective	Includes all criteria Main idea and flow of ideas are clear and presented in a focused, coherent manner Has an effective introduction and conclusion	
	Uses time poorly; the whole presentation, or a part of it, is too short or too long	Generally times presentation well, but may spend too much or too little time on a topic	Organizes time well; no part is rushed, too short, or too long	
Presentation Aids	Does not use audio/visual aids or media Attempts to use one or a few audio/visual aids or media but they distract from or do not add to the presentation	Uses audio/visual aids or media, but they sometimes distract from or do not add to the presentation	Uses well-produced audio/visual aids or media to clarify information, emphasize important points, strengthen arguments, and add interest	
Response to Audience Questions	Does not address audience questions or misunderstands without seeking clarification	Answers some audience questions, but not always clearly or completely	Answers audience questions clearly and completely Seeks clarification when needed and explains how the answer might be found when unable to answer a question	
Participation in Team Presentations	Not all team members participate; only one or two speak	All team members participate, but not equally	All team members participate for about the same length of time All team members are able to answer questions about the topic as a whole, not just their part of it	

INTERNET RESOURCES

National Geographic's "7 Billion" video

- *www.youtube.com/watch?v=sc4HxPxNrZ0*

National Geographic's "Invasive Species 101" video

- *www.youtube.com/watch?v=gYNAtw1c7hI*

Invasive species information

- National Invasive Species Information Center –*www.invasivespeciesinfo.gov/unitedstates/state.shtml*

- Exotic Pest Detection by State – *http://pest.ceris.purdue.edu/states.php*

- USGS: Nonindigenous Aquatic Species –*http://nas.er.usgs.gov/queries/StateSearch.aspx*

- USDA: State Noxious Weed Lists –*www.ams.usda.gov/sites/default/files/media/StateNoxiousWeedsSeedList.pdf*

Population counting methods

- *www.geographynotes.com/wildlife-census/how-to-conduct-wildlife-census-3-methods-geography/5963*

- *https://open.oregonstate.education/monitoring/chapter/field-techniques-for-population-sampling-and-estimation/*

- *http://scientistatwork.blogs.nytimes.com/2011/05/03/three-ways-to-count-whales/?_r=0*

- *https://cires.colorado.edu/outreach/sites/default/files/2021-01/Population%20Estimates%20Teacher%20Guide.pdf*

- *https://adfg.alaska.gov/index.cfm?adfg=wildlifenews.view_article&articles_id=814*

Population Education's "World of 7 Billion" activities

- *www.worldof7billion.org/teacher-resources/middle-school-activities/*

Population growth issues

- *https://ugc.berkeley.edu/background-content/population-growth/*

- *www.un.org/en/desa/population-growth-environmental-degradation-and-climate-change*

Scientist in the Field book series

- *www.sciencemeetsadventure.com/books/*

US Census history

- *www.census.gov/history/pdf/cff4.pdf*

US Census "Quick Facts"

- www.census.gov/quickfacts

"Wild Marlborough – Asian Long Horned Beetles" video

- *www.youtube.com/watch?t=168&v=ERC4m90cxjU*

TRANSFORMING LEARNING WITH GLOBAL POPULATION ISSUES AND THE *STEM ROAD MAP CURRICULUM SERIES*

Carla C. Johnson

This chapter serves as a conclusion to the Global Population Issues integrated STEM curriculum module, but it is just the beginning of the transformation of your classroom that is possible through use of the *STEM Road Map Curriculum Series*. In this book, many key resources have been provided to make learning meaningful for your students through integration of science, technology, engineering, and mathematics, as well as social studies and English language arts, into powerful problem- and project-based instruction. The Global Population Issues curriculum is grounded in the latest theory of learning for students in grade 7 specifically. Students acquire important knowledge and skills grounded in national academic standards in mathematics, English language arts, science, and 21st century skills that will enable their learning to be deeper, retained longer, and applied throughout, illustrating the critical connections within and across disciplines. Finally, authentic formative assessments, including strategies for differentiation and addressing misconceptions, are embedded within the curriculum activities.

The Global Population Issues curriculum in the **Sustainable Systems** STEM Road Map theme can be used in single-content classrooms (e.g., mathematics) where there is only one teacher or expanded to include multiple teachers and content areas across classrooms. Through the exploration of the Global Population Issues lesson plans, students engage in a real-world STEM problem on the first day of instruction and gather necessary knowledge and skills along the way in the context of solving the problem.

The other topics in the *STEM Road Map Curriculum Series* are designed in a similar manner, and NSTA Press and Routledge have published additional volumes in this series for this and other grade levels, and have plans to publish more.

For an up-to-date list of volumes in the series, please visit *www.routledge.com/STEM-Road-Map-Curriculum-Series/book-series/SRM* (for titles co-published by Routledge and

NSTA Press), or *www.nsta.org/book-series/stem-road-map-curriculum* (for titles published by NSTA Press).

If you are interested in professional development opportunities focused on the STEM Road Map specifically or integrated STEM or STEM programs and schools overall, contact the lead editor of this project, Dr. Carla C. Johnson, Professor of Science Education at NC State University. Someone from the team will be in touch to design a program that will meet your individual, school, or district needs.

APPENDIX

CONTENT STANDARDS ADDRESSED IN THIS MODULE

NEXT GENERATION SCIENCE STANDARDS

Table A1 lists the science and engineering practices, disciplinary core ideas, and cross-cutting concepts this module addresses. The supported performance expectations are as follows:

- MS-LS1–6. Construct a scientific explanation based on evidence for the role of photosynthesis in the cycling of matter and flow of energy into and out of organisms.

- MS-LS1–7. Develop a model to describe how food is rearranged through chemical reactions forming new molecules that support growth and/or release energy as this matter moves through an organism.

- MS-LS2-1. Analyze and interpret data to provide evidence for the effects of resource availability on organisms and populations of organisms in an ecosystem.

- MS-LS2-2. Construct an explanation that predicts patterns of interactions among organisms across multiple ecosystems.

- MS-LS2–3. Develop a model to describe the cycling of matter and flow of energy among living and nonliving parts of an ecosystem.

- MS-LS2–4. Construct an argument supported by empirical evidence that changes to physical or biological components of an ecosystem affect populations.

Table A.1 Next Generation Science Standards (NGSS)

Science and Engineering Practices
DEVELOPING AND USING MODELS • Develop and use a model to describe phenomena. • Develop a model to describe unobservable mechanisms. OBTAINING, EVALUATING, AND COMMUNICATING INFORMATION • Gather, read, and synthesize information from multiple appropriate sources and assess the credibility, accuracy, and possible bias of each publication and methods used, and describe how they are supported or not supported by evidence. ANALYZING AND INTERPRETING DATA • Analyze and interpret data to provide evidence for phenomena. CONSTRUCTING EXPLANATIONS AND DESIGNING SOLUTIONS • Construct a scientific explanation based on valid and reliable evidence obtained from sources (including the students' own experiments) and the assumption that theories and laws that describe the natural world operate today as they did in the past and will continue to do so in the future. ENGAGING IN ARGUMENT FROM EVIDENCE • Construct and present oral and written arguments supported by empirical evidence and scientific reasoning to support or refute an explanation or a model for a phenomenon or a solution to a problem.
Disciplinary Core Ideas
LS1.C: ORGANIZATION FOR MATTER AND ENERGY FLOW IN ORGANISMS • Plants, algae (including phytoplankton), and many microorganisms use the energy from light to make sugars (food) from carbon dioxide from the atmosphere and water through the process of photosynthesis, which also releases oxygen. These sugars can be used immediately or stored for growth or later use. • Within individual organisms, food moves through a series of chemical reactions in which it is broken down and rearranged to form new molecules, to support growth, or to release energy. LS2.A: INTERDEPENDENT RELATIONSHIPS IN ECOSYSTEMS • Organisms, and populations of organisms, are dependent on their environmental interactions both with other living things and with nonliving factors. • In any ecosystem, organisms and populations with similar requirements for food, water, oxygen, or other resources may compete with each other for limited resources, access to which consequently constrains their growth and reproduction. • Growth of organisms and population increases are limited by access to resources. LS2.B: CYCLE OF MATTER AND ENERGY TRANSFER IN ECOSYSTEMS • Food webs are models that demonstrate how matter and energy is transferred between producers, consumers, and decomposers as the three groups interact within an ecosystem. Transfers of matter into and out of the physical environment occur at every level. Decomposers recycle nutrients from dead plant or animal matter back to the soil in terrestrial environments or to the water in aquatic environments. The atoms that make up the organisms in an ecosystem are cycled repeatedly between the living and nonliving parts of the ecosystem. LS2.C: ECOSYSTEM DYNAMICS, FUNCTIONING, AND RESILIENCE • Ecosystems are dynamic in nature; their characteristics can vary over time. Disruptions to any physical or biological component of an ecosystem can lead to shifts in all its populations. PS3.D: ENERGY IN CHEMICAL PROCESSES AND EVERYDAY LIFE • The chemical reaction by which plants produce complex food molecules (sugars) requires an energy input (i.e., from sunlight) to occur. In this reaction, carbon dioxide and water combine to form carbon-based organic molecules and release oxygen. • Cellular respiration in plants and animals involve chemical reactions with oxygen that release stored energy. In these processes, complex molecules containing carbon react with oxygen to produce carbon dioxide and other materials.

Crosscutting Concepts
CAUSE AND EFFECT • Cause and effect relationships may be used to predict phenomena in natural or designed systems. ENERGY AND MATTER • Within a natural system, the transfer of energy drives the motion and/or cycling of matter. • Matter is conserved because atoms are conserved in physical and chemical processes. • The transfer of energy can be tracked as energy flows through a natural system. STABILITY AND CHANGE • Small changes in one part of a system might cause large changes in another part. SCIENTIFIC KNOWLEDGE ASSUMES AN ORDER AND CONSISTENCY IN NATURAL SYSTEMS • Science assumes that objects and events in natural systems occur in consistent patterns that are understandable through measurement and observation.

Source: NGSS Lead States. (2013). *Next Generation Science Standards: For states, by states.* National Academies Press. www.nextgenscience.org/next-generation-science-standards.

Table A.2 Common Core Mathematics and English/Language Arts Standards

Common Core State Mathematics Standards	Common Core State English Language Arts (ELA) Standards
MATHEMATICAL PRACTICES • MP1. Make sense of problems and persevere in solving them. • MP2. Reason abstractly and quantitatively. • MP3. Construct viable arguments and critique the reasoning of others. • MP4. Model with mathematics. • MP5. Use appropriate tools strategically. • MP6. Attend to precision. • MP8. Look for and express regularity in repeated reasoning. MATHEMATICAL CONTENT • 7.SP.A.1. Understand that statistics can be used to gain information about a population by examining a sample of the population; generalizations about a population from a sample are valid only if the sample is representative of that population. Understand that random sampling tends to produce representative samples and support valid inferences.	READING STANDARDS • RI.7.8. Trace and evaluate the argument and specific claims in a text, assessing whether the reasoning is sound and the evidence is relevant and sufficient to support the claims. • RI.7.9. Analyze how two or more authors writing about the same topic shape their presentations of key information by emphasizing different evidence or advancing different interpretations of facts. WRITING STANDARDS • W.7.1. Write arguments to support claims with clear reasons and relevant evidence. • W.7.1.a. Introduce claim(s), acknowledge alternate or opposing claims, and organize the reasons and evidence logically. • W.7.1.b. Support claim(s) with logical reasoning and relevant evidence, using accurate, credible sources and demonstrating an understanding of the topic or text. • W.7.1.c. Use words, phrases, and clauses to create cohesion and clarify the relationships among claim(s), reasons, and evidence. • W.7.1.e. Provide a concluding statement or section that follows from and supports the argument presented. • W.7.2. Write informative/explanatory texts to examine a topic and convey ideas, concepts, and information through the selection, organization, and analysis of relevant content.

Table A.2 (*continued*)

Common Core State Mathematics Standards	Common Core State English Language Arts (ELA) Standards
• 7.SP.A.2. Use data from a random sample to draw inferences about a population with an unknown characteristic of interest. Generate multiple samples (or simulated samples) of the same size to gauge the variation in estimates or predictions. For example, estimate the mean word length in a book by randomly sampling words from the book; predict the winner of a school election based on randomly sampled survey data. Gauge how far off the estimate or prediction might be. • 7.SP.B.3. Informally assess the degree of visual overlap of two numerical data distributions with similar variabilities, measuring the difference between the centers by expressing it as a multiple of a measure of variability. • 7.SP.B.4. Use measures of center and measures of variability for numerical data from random samples to draw informal comparative inferences about two populations. • 7.RP.A.2. Recognize and represent proportional relationships between quantities.	• W.7.2.a. Introduce a topic clearly, previewing what is to follow; organize ideas, concepts, and information, using strategies such as definition, classification, comparison/contrast, and cause/effect; include formatting (e.g., headings), graphics (e.g., charts, tables), and multimedia when useful to aiding comprehension. • W.7.2.b. Develop the topic with relevant facts, definitions, concrete details, quotations, or other information and examples. • W.7.2.d. Use precise language and domain-specific vocabulary to inform about or explain the topic. • W.7.3.c. Use a variety of transition words, phrases, and clauses to convey sequence and signal shifts from one time frame or setting to another. • W.7.6. Use technology, including the Internet, to produce and publish writing and link to and cite sources as well as to interact and collaborate with others, including linking to and citing sources. • W.7.7. Conduct short research projects to answer a question, drawing on several sources and generating additional related, focused questions for further research and investigation. • W.7.8. Gather relevant information from multiple print and digital sources, using search terms effectively; assess the credibility and accuracy of each source; and quote or paraphrase the data and conclusions of others while avoiding plagiarism and following a standard format for citation. • W.7.9. Draw evidence from literary or informational texts to support analysis, reflection, and research. SPEAKING AND LISTENING STANDARDS • SL.7.1. Engage effectively in a range of collaborative discussions (one-on-one, in groups, and teacher-led) with diverse partners on grade 7 topics, texts, and issues, building on others' ideas and expressing their own clearly. • SL.7.1.a. Come to discussions prepared, having read or researched material under study; explicitly draw on that preparation by referring to evidence on the topic, text, or issue to probe and reflect on ideas under discussion. • SL.7.1.b. Follow rules for collegial discussions, track progress toward specific goals and deadlines, and define individual roles as needed. • SL.7.1.c. Pose questions that elicit elaboration and respond to others' questions and comments with relevant observations and ideas that bring the discussion back on topic as needed. • SL.7.1.d. Acknowledge new information expressed by others and, when warranted, modify their own views.

Table A.2 (*continued*)

Common Core State Mathematics Standards	Common Core State English Language Arts (ELA) Standards
	• SL.7.3. Delineate a speaker's argument and specific claims, evaluating the soundness of the reasoning and the relevance and sufficiency of the evidence. • SL.7.4. Present claims and findings, emphasizing salient points in a focused, coherent manner with pertinent descriptions, facts, details, and examples; use appropriate eye contact, adequate volume, and clear pronunciation. • SL.7.5. Include multimedia components and visual displays in presentations to clarify claims and findings and emphasize salient points.

Table A.3 21st Century Skills Addressed in STEM Road Map Module (www.p21.org)

21st Century Skills	Learning Skills and Technology Tools (from P21 framework)	Teaching Strategies	Evidence of Success
Interdisciplinary themes	• Global Awareness • Environmental Literacy • Civic Literacy • Financial, Economic, Business, and Entrepreneurial Literacy	• Draw connections between population density and geographical, natural, social, demographic, political, and historical features. • Highlight the psychological, physical, and environmental impacts of population density on humans and other species.	• Students will analyze and interpret data from maps, data tables, and infographics to make and test conjectures about the population of a region. • Students will also explore some ways that scientists, technology experts, engineers, and mathematicians are addressing the issue of overpopulation and population density.
Learning and Innovation Skills	• Creativity and Innovation • Critical Thinking and Problem Solving • Communication and Collaboration	• Examine urban planning issues associated with overpopulation. • Examine the advantages and disadvantages of sampling techniques. • Facilitate group work, students' development of a mathematical model, and use of presentation tools/software.	• Students will create a mathematical model that will provide an accurate estimate of the population of their assigned species. • Students will present their mathematical model to a panel of experts.

Table A.3 (*continued*)

21st Century Skills	Learning Skills and Technology Tools (from P21 framework)	Teaching Strategies	Evidence of Success
Information, Media and Technology Skills	• Information Literacy • Media Literacy • ICT Literacy	• Have students use nonfiction text to research sampling techniques and develop their mathematical model. • Help students use multimedia tools to present their findings.	• Students present to peers, teachers, and a panel of experts using multimedia tools. • Students' reflection on the use of nonfiction text. • Student completion of digital stories.
Life and Career Skills	• Flexibility and Adaptability; Initiative and Self-Direction • Social and Cross Cultural Skills • Productivity and Accountability • Leadership and Responsibility	• Provide guidelines for effective peer critique and how to use this feedback to improve presentation. • Establish collaborative learning expectations. • Scaffold completion of tasks.	• Students complete mathematical model presentations on time with evidence of collaboration by the whole group.

Source: Partnership for 21st Century Learning. (2015). Framework for 21st Century Learning. www.p21.org/our-work/p21-framework.

Table A.4 English Language Development Standards Addressed in STEM Road Map Module

English Language Development Standards: Grades 6–8 (WIDA, 2012)
ELD Standard 1: Social and Instructional Language English language learners communicate for Social and Instructional purposes within the school setting. ELD Standard 2: The Language of Language Arts English language learners communicate information, ideas, and concepts necessary for academic success in the content area of Language Arts. ELD Standard 3: The Language of Mathematics English language learners communicate information, ideas, and concepts necessary for academic success in the content area of Mathematics. ELD Standard 4: The Language of Science English language learners communicate information, ideas, and concepts necessary for academic success in the content area of Science. ELD Standard 5: The Language of Social Studies English language learners communicate information, ideas, and concepts necessary for academic success in the content area of Social Studies.

Source: WIDA. (2012). 2012 amplification of the English language development standards: Kindergarten–grade 12. *www.wida.us/standards/eld.aspx*.

INDEX

Note: **Bold** page numbers refer to tables

For Product Safety Concerns and Information please contact our EU
representative GPSR@taylorandfrancis.com Taylor & Francis Verlag GmbH,
Kaufingerstraße 24, 80331 München, Germany

Batch number: 08151882

Printed by Printforce, the Netherlands